International Congregational Council

The Boston Book

containing matter relating to the second International Congregational Council, at Boston, Massachusetts, U.S.A., 20-28 September, 1899, including the program and list of officers and delegates

International Congregational Council

The Boston Book

containing matter relating to the second International Congregational council, at Boston, Massachusetts, U.S.A., 20-28 September, 1899, including the program and list of officers and delegates

ISBN/EAN: 9783337302030

Printed in Europe, USA, Canada, Australia, Japan

Cover: Foto ©Suzi / pixelio.de

More available books at **www.hansebooks.com**

The Boston Book

Containing matter relating to the **SECOND INTERNATIONAL CONGREGATIONAL COUNCIL,** at Boston, Massachusetts, U.S.A., 20-28 September, 1899, including the Program and list of Officers and Delegates; together with sketches of Boston and an account of its Congregational activities and some reference to other near-by points of Pilgrim and Puritan interest

14 Beacon Street, BOSTON, Massachusetts

The Congregationalist

MDCCCXCIX

THE CONGREGATIONALIST

EIGHTY-THREE years of vigorous life entitle a religious newspaper to a place among the important institutions of a city or a nation. *The Congregationalist* claims the honor of being the oldest journal of its class in the world, and throughout its long career it has been a constant and potent factor in the life of multitudes. With the changing years, its external appearance has undergone great transformation. The contents of the paper, too, have been continually broadened and diversified in order to keep pace with the best life of the world. But through all change and advance, the animating purpose has been to emphasize the things of the spiritual life and of the Kingdom of God.

To-day *The Congregationalist* is better equipped for its work than ever before. With a staff of seven editors, who give all their time to the work of the office, with specialists in charge of various departments, with consulting editors in several States, with correspondents in important centers and in foreign lands as well, and with many writers of international repute, it has every facility for the making of a strong, well-balanced, and interesting paper. It invites the examination of all who believe that the distinctly religious journal, despite the multiplication of excellent periodicals of many kinds, is still an essential element in the life of every growing Christian. Grateful for the oft-expressed appreciation of its increasing army of readers, *The Congregationalist* faces the new century with a determination to render a larger service than ever before.

Subscription Rates.— *In advance, 1 year, $3.00; 2 years, $5.00; 5 years, $10.00. Club of* FIVE, *one at least being new, $10.00. This special rate of $2.00 is also available for Church Clubs under certain conditions. On trial, to a new address, 3 months, 25 cts.; 6 months, $1.00. Four sample copies free.*

THE CONGREGATIONALIST, *14 Beacon Street, Boston, Mass., U. S. A.*

H. GAZE & SONS

BEG leave to announce to the members of The International Congregational Council their high-class conducted parties to **Egypt and the Holy Land,** including a trip up the Nile and special facilities in Palestine; a tour **Around the World** of a very comprehensive nature, unsurpassed by any ever attempted; and many others to **England and The Continent,** allowing a variety of routes and meeting individual tastes and purses.

First-class steamers and accommodations, good hotels, and the best of service are guaranteed, and *all necessary expenses* are included in the stipulated cost of the tour.

The business arrangements and conduct of both of THE CONGREGATIONALIST Parties, the **Holy Land Tour** of 1895, and the **Pilgrimage to England and Holland** of 1897, were intrusted to us by the proprietors of that paper. These were two of the most successful special tours ever organized.

We also have exceptional facilities for furnishing tickets and hotel coupons for individual travel anywhere. Passengers traveling under our system have the advantage of being able to apply to our numerous branch managers and agents in the principal cities in different parts of the world, for local information or other attention during their tour abroad.

Send for descriptive circular, stating tour desired.

H. GAZE & SONS.

W. H. EAVES, *New England Ag't,*   R. H. CRUNDEN, *Gen'l Manager,*
201 Washington St., Boston.   113 Broadway, New York.

PART I

Boston and About

Pilgrim Sight-seer in Boston	9	Pilgrim Sight-seer In Newe' Towne	
Boston Congregational Churches	21	(Cambridge and Newton)	51
Boston City Missions	29	Pilgrim Sight-seer in Salem	61
Congregationalism in Greater Boston,	30	Pilgrim Sight-seer in Plymouth	77
Other Denominations in Boston	34	Pilgrim Sight-seer in Andover	89
Literary and Educational Boston	39	Pilgrim Sight-seer in Concord and Lexington	96
Short Trips about Boston	46		
Pilgrim Sight-seer's Directory	161	The Congregational House	112
		Congregational Societies	121-132

PART II
The International Council,
pages 133-160

PART III
Illustrations and Business Information,
pages 163-232

BOSTON FROM THE EDITORIAL WINDOWS OF THE CONGREGATONALIST.

THE PILGRIM SIGHT-SEER IN BOSTON

The most picturesque of American cities, the richest in historic associations, the heart of the Puritan Commonwealth, is Boston. From what place can the visitor best begin to study and enjoy its points of interest? Near to the center of its most important historic localities, of its government and much of its wealth and culture, is the Congregational House, on Beacon Hill. The offices of *The Congregationalist* overlook Boston, its harbor and surrounding country.

It is easy, from this point, to mark the outlines of the ancient town. In its center, near the head of State Street, stood the meeting-house of the First Church, erected in 1631. In that year the court at Charlestown ordered that Trimountain be called Boston. The second, or North, dedicated in 1650, stood yonder on North Square, at the North End. The third, or South, erected in 1670, stood where the Old South meeting-house now stands, at the head of Milk Street, at the South End. The early settlers drove their cows to pasture on the slopes of Beacon Hill and on the Common. They carted their grain to be ground into flour in the windmill on Copp's Hill or the mill at the foot of Summer Street. Beside the cart-paths and the cow-paths houses were built from time to time, till the crooked streets were outlined. Old Boston was not planned — it grew.

Next to Plymouth Rock and its surroundings, no place is so dear to American Congregationalists as that now before us. John Cotton, the famous pastor of the First Church from 1633, who has been called the spiritual father of Boston, lived on and owned a portion of what is now Pemberton Square. Increase Mather lived on North Street, and Cotton Mather on Hanover Street — father and son, pastors of North Church.

OLD SOUTH MEETING HOUSE.

The Pilgrim Sight-seer in Boston

Next to the Old South meeting-house was the residence of John Winthrop, the most renowned governor of Massachusetts Bay Colony. This whole region is crowded with sites of the homesteads of famous families and with spots where events of great historic interest occurred.

But with our limited space we must confine our attention to landmarks still standing. At the head of State Street, on Washington, is the Old State House, built in 1748, on the site of the Town House, built in 1657. John Adams said that here Independence was born. It would require columns to give a list of the great events of colonial history which occurred here. But its historic tablets and its museum of relics and antiquities are open to visitors daily. The museum of the Old South meeting-house, a few steps away, must not be passed unvisited. Close at hand is School Street, near the head of which the Latin School stood for more than 200 years, where Franklin, Hancock, Adams, Otis, Sumner, Henry Ward Beecher, and a long list of other famous men studied. Next to it was, and still is, King's Chapel, on the site of the First Episcopal Church in Boston. The present building is 150 years old and has an interesting interior. The Burial Ground beside it is the oldest in the city, and here Winthrop and other colonial governors, with John Cotton, John Davenport, and many other eminent clergymen, judges, and merchants, were laid to rest. Two minutes' walk brings you to the Granary Burial Ground, which surpasses all the others in the number of its distinguished dead. Here lie the remains of John Hancock, Samuel Adams, James Otis, Paul Revere, Peter Faneuil, Judge Samuel Sewall, the parents of Benjamin Franklin, and a long list of names renowned in colonial history. It was named from the Granary, a great building for the storage of grain reserved to be sold to the poor at cost. It stood on the site now occupied by Park Street Church.

The Pilgrim Sight-seer in Boston

Not far away, off Washington Street, in what is now known as Province Court, stood the old Province House for nearly two centuries, in colonial times the residence of vice-regal governors. Burned down in 1864, its walls still remain in other buildings on the same site. Returning now to the Old State House, we pass into Dock Square, facing Faneuil Hall. This is "The Cradle of Liberty" which, since before the Revolution, has been the scene of many famous meetings in behalf of patriotism, reforms, and other public movements. It is opened for assemblies whenever, under certain conditions, a request is made, signed by fifty citizens. Many a memorable oration has been delivered from that platform. Portraits of famous men adorn its walls. It is open daily to visitors. A look at Faneuil and Quincy Markets is well worth a half hour's tarry before leaving this neighborhood.

Returning again toward the Congregational House, one may see the statues of Samuel Adams in Adams Square, of John Winthrop in Scollay Square, and of Benjamin Franklin in School Street, in front of the City Hall. A short detour will bring you to Christ Church on Salem Street, the oldest church edifice in the city. It was built in 1723, and its interior has many quaint relics. From its tower the signal lights of Paul Revere were hung, and here General Gage witnessed the battle of Bunker Hill, whose tall monument, across in Charlestown, invites a visit. Near the church is Copp's Hill, whose burial ground contains the tombs of the Mathers and other honored families.

We must turn from historic places, without even having named many that Bostonians love to linger over, and regard the Boston of to-day. Once more in the street by the Congregational House, we study for a few moments the four historic tablets on its façade which tell so well the story of the foundations of the Commonwealth laid by the Pilgrims and the

CHRIST CHURCH.

The Pilgrim Sight-seer in Boston

Puritans — Law, Religion, Education, Philanthropy. Opposite is the headquarters of the Unitarian denomination, which in the early part of this century appropriated so large a portion of the material heritage of Congregationalists. Next door is the Athenæum, with its wealth of literature. Next block to the north, past the buildings of Boston University, is the magnificent Suffolk County Court House, costing nearly four million dollars. Its rotunda, with fine frescoes and sculptures, invites inspection. On Tremont Street, near the end of Beacon, is Tremont Temple, the Baptist headquarters, where most of the meetings of the International Congregational Council are to be held. On the summit of Beacon Hill stands the State House, with its new addition completed, its gilded dome glistening in the sun by day and crowned with electric lights at night. Dr. Holmes called it the Hub of the solar system, but that was before the system of electric lighting was invented. It contains the first State library in America, and its busts and statues and flags and trophies and portraits will require considerable time and repay thoughtful study. Here may be seen the original manuscript of William Bradford's history of Plymouth Colony, known in England as the Log of the *Mayflower*, and returned to this country in 1897 by the Consistory Court of the Diocese of London.

Leaving the State House grounds and entering the Common, we pass the Shaw Monument, St. Gaudens' masterpiece, around which some interested spectators are nearly always standing. Nothing in the city is more characteristic of its spirit than this monument to the brave officer who died in the Civil War at the head of his regiment of negroes. Colonel Shaw belonged to one of the first families of Boston. He took the command of negro troops when the position involved much obloquy and sacrifice. You are now in the famous park which is the pride of all Bostonians. Recall the great open-air meetings, the

STATE HOUSE IN WINTER.

reviews of armies, the hangings of Quakers, and the revivals under Whitfield's preaching which have taken place on these grounds, once a great pasture field covered with stones and huckleberry bushes, now a splendid expanse of hill and valley with noble elms and shady walks. Pass down the long path by the Frog Pond. Let us choose an afternoon when the fountain is playing. Visit the statues and monuments. Pause beside the old burying ground, where were laid the bodies of a number of officers and soldiers of the Revolution. Watch the games on the playground. Then cross the street into the Public Garden, with its shade trees, parterres of flower beds, its shrubbery, its pretty lake with boats and bridges. Follow with your eyes the long vista down the broad Commonwealth Avenue, lined with noble buildings, stretching far to the entrance of the Fenway and a part of the magnificent system of parks and parkway encircling the city, unsurpassed in this country, or perhaps anywhere in the world.

Over the buildings to the south rise many church spires, for the best residence portion of the city has been for many years steadily moving westward. At the corner of Marlboro Street stands the edifice of the First Church in Boston, whose name and property passed to the Unitarians.

Walking from the Public Garden down Boylston Street, we approach Copley Square. Just before reaching it, we pass the fine building of the Young Men's Christian Association. Just beyond are the Natural History Museum and the buildings of the Massachusetts Institute of Technology, the leading college in America of industrial sciences. Here are given annually courses of free lectures of the Lowell Institute, by prominent American and British scholars. Copley Square itself, named from Boston's greatest artist, is surrounded by the finest buildings, with the most superb architecture in New England. On the southeast is Trinity Church, Episcopalian, with ivy-covered

From Guide to Metropolitan Boston
Copyright, 1899, Geo. H. Walker & Co.

The Pilgrim Sight-seer in Boston

granite and sandstone walls, a Galilee porch adorned with bas-reliefs, cloisters containing stone tracery from a window of St. Botolph's, in Boston, England, and a massive central tower 211 feet high. This building is the masterpiece of the noted architect, Mr. H. H. Richardson. It was erected when Phillips Brooks was rector of the church. On the south side of the square is the Museum of Fine Arts, with one of the finest sets of sculptured casts in the world, and an unrivaled Japanese collection. Its paintings by old and modern masters, its porcelain and glass ware, classic and Renaissance statuary, Egyptian and Cyprus collections, give it the first rank among art museums in America. On the west side is the Boston Public Library, one of the costliest and finest buildings of its kind in the world, and containing the largest city library in the world for free circulation. It was finished in 1895, at a cost of $2,500,000. The funds were furnished by the State, the city, and by private gifts. Here the humblest citizen can have free access to the leading newspapers of the world and to more than 700,000 volumes of books, while he can enjoy masterpieces of architecture, sculpture, and painting, united in one of the most splendid palaces in the world. Robert C. Winthrop happily named it Boston's Literary Common. On the north side of the square, nearly opposite to Trinity, is a Gothic brownstone edifice with the inscription "The Second Church in Boston. Founded 1649." The Congregational church of the Mathers and Emerson, now Unitarian, has here erected its home. On the corner of Dartmouth Street, occupying the most conspicuous position, and the pioneer building in Copley Square, is the meeting-house of the New Old South Church. Its square tower, with open Gothic windows, is one of the most beautiful in existence. It is 248 feet high. This, the Third Church, by a majority of one vote, was held to the faith of its founders during the controversy in the early part of this century when all the other his-

PUBLIC LIBRARY AND OLD SOUTH CHURCH

From Guide to Metropolitan Boston
Copyright, 1899, Geo. H. Walker & Co.

toric Congregational churches became Unitarian. The large property which it inherited and its wealthy membership have enabled it to stand first among our churches in its benefactions to sister churches and to the missionary work of the denomination.

Beginning our tour from Beacon Hill, in the new Congregational House, looking down on the heart of the ancient town, we end in the new portion of the city, standing in its finest square and under the shadow of its noblest church tower, which belongs to the leading Congregational church of Boston. We have passed without mention many scenes of deep historic interest, and a great wealth of public and private buildings. We have had no space to describe the Young Women's Christian Association, the interesting college settlements, and the many mission and philanthropic enterprises —which purify and bless the city. We have left unnoticed abounding evidences of commercial enterprise, of civic pride, and of private generosity for public good. We have been unable even to glance at our beautiful harbor or at the suburbs surrounding the city, on every side attractive. We have written as a citizen and a Congregationalist, a lover of our city, past and present, accompanying friends on their first visit, whom we would gladly persuade to return for a more leisurely and minute study of the Edinburgh of America.

BOSTON CONGREGATIONAL CHURCHES

In the inner sections of the city, Congregationalism has for many years been represented by seven organizations, all but one — Park Street — having occupied two and in some cases three different sites. That exception is now the only strictly down-town church, and while Park Street has a distinct mission to the numerous hotels and boarding houses in its neighborhood and to the floating population that gathers around the heart of the busy section of any great city, it also continues to be the spiritual home of many persons who have removed into the suburbs, but who still resort to it Sunday by Sunday. It has always stood for the distinctly orthodox type of theology, having been born in the midst of the Unitarian controversy as a protest against the drift toward liberal thought which was then so marked in many of the other churches. Park Street has a splendid missionary record, many of our workers on foreign soil having been ordained within its walls, and many large gifts having come from the members. It is a popular rallying place for religious meetings, being so accessible from all parts of the city. Its pastor is Rev. J. L. Withrow, D.D.

In the Back Bay are the Old South, the Central, and the Mt. Vernon churches. The first has the distinction of being the richest church of our denomination in the city, and its Christian liberality can bear comparison with its reputed wealth. Its beautiful and costly edifice fitly adorns one of the noblest squares in the city. During the fall and winter months it is usually thronged, not only by the resident constituency, but by many strangers, drawn by the fame of its pastor, Rev. George A. Gordon, D.D. The music is of a character befitting the standing of the church. It sustains a flourishing mission in a thickly populated section.

PARK STREET CHURCH.

Boston Congregational Churches

Not more than two or three blocks from the Old South Church is Central Church, whose lofty spire is thought by many to be the finest in the city. Within this noble example of Gothic architecture are fittings and adornments of the most churchly character. They represent a large outlay of time and strength on the part of the present pastor, Rev. E. L. Clark, D.D., as well as the unstinted generosity of his people, who have sought to make this sanctuary one of dignity and worth. The stained-glass windows, the work of the best artists and workmen in this country, will repay attentive study. The furnishings of the pulpit, the massive chandelier, the coloring — in fact, all the elements which contribute to the unity of impression will be appreciated by all who believe that the house of the Lord should be as perfect as the means at hand can make it. A rich form of worship is carried out at each service.

Further out on the Back Bay, at the junction of Beacon Street and Massachusetts Avenue, and almost abutting on the handsome Harvard Bridge which crosses the Charles, is Mt. Vernon Church, where Rev. S. E. Herrick, D.D., has preached sermons of remarkable force and finish for over twenty-five years. This church once occupied the edifice on Ashburton Place now metamorphosed into the Boston University Law School, and it was here that Dwight L. Moody attended church when he was a clerk in Boston. Its change of location has not weakened its hold upon its loyal constituency, and has proved favorable to the coming in of others residing in its present vicinage.

At the South End our denomination has three exponents, each not far from the other, but each possessing a worthy history and doing a distinctive work. Berkeley Temple is easily distinguished from afar by its bright red hue. It is the largest church of the denomination, not only in the city, but in New England, having now over twelve hundred mem-

CENTRAL CHURCH.

bers. During the last ten years it has become nationally known as foremost among so-called institutional churches, supplementing its preaching and evangelistic work by varied forms of ministry to the social, æsthetic, and intellectual nature. It is a hive of industries from the beginning of the week to the close, and the young and unattached persons in the South End respond to the provision for their comfort and growth through reading rooms, clubs, and classes. Rev. C. A. Dickinson, D.D., is pastor, and Rev. W. S. Kelsey, associate.

Shawmut Church was once one of the most popular and fashionable in the city, but the church-sustaining population has largely drifted into other sections of the city and to the suburbs. Enough stout hearts and capable hands remain in the present membership of the church to sustain a vigorous people's work. The free pew system is in force here as at Berkeley Temple, and in other ways the church undertakes to become an attractive center, and one whose wholesome influence shall be felt particularly by the students who sojourn for a longer or shorter while in that part of the city. Rev. W. T. McElveen, PH.D., has been the pastor since last March. Rev. E. B. Webb, D.D., is the honored pastor *emeritus*. The organ is one of the finest in the city, and the auditorium, for size and acoustic properties, has few equals anywhere.

The third South End church, Union, is also blessed with a commodious and handsome house of worship. It is still a church of the family type, though it, too, like its neighbors, draws to itself many of the floating class, and infuses into them a spirit of loyalty and readiness for work. The pastor, Rev. S. L. Loomis, D.D., is the author of a book on "Modern Cities and Their Problems."

In Roxbury, one of the pleasant residential outskirts of the city, are no less than five Congregational churches. The

SECOND CHURCH, DORCHESTER.

mother of them all is Eliot, where Rev. A. C. Thompson, D.D., has been pastor since 1842, but of late years the active work has been carried on by a colleague. This church has contributed its very lifeblood for the starting of other organizations. Its children, however, rise up to call it blessed and do it honor. The oldest is Immanuel, of which Rev. C. H. Beale, D.D., is pastor. Then comes the Highland, Rev. W. R. Campbell, and Walnut Avenue, where Rev. A. H. Plumb, D.D., has shepherded a devoted people for twenty-seven years. The Olivet Church is not far away. In fields which are becoming every day more heterogeneous, these churches are doing excellent and durable work. Still further out, at West Roxbury, Rev. F. W. Merrick is pastor of a homogeneous and vigorous suburban church.

Jamaica Plain has two flourishing churches — the Central, Rev. C. L. Morgan, D.D., pastor, and Boylston, Rev. Ellis Mendell; while at Roslindale is one of our newer churches.

In Dorchester the old Second Church looms up as one of the strongest and most influential in the entire Boston circle. Its roots go down deep into the early life of that section of the city, and its prominent leaders have been identified with the broader concerns of the denomination. Rev. Arthur Little, D.D., is pastor.

Another strong Dorchester church is the Pilgrim, of which Rev. W. H. Allbright, D.D., is pastor, under whom it has had a wonderful development, exhibiting to-day a virility and unity which go far to justify an outsider's recent characterization of it as the "most successful church in Boston." It exercises parental care over a new enterprise — the Romsey Street Chapel. Other sections of Dorchester are well ministered to by the Harvard Church, Rev. W. T. Beale, pastor, the Village, Rev. G. W. Brooks, pastor, the Central, and Trinity.

On the western borders of the city, Brighton and Allston, Congregationalism is creditably represented by the church at

Brighton over which Rev. A. A. Berle, D.D., presides, and at Allston by that of which Rev. J. O. Haarvig is pastor. These are strong plants, and adequate to the demands made on them.

In South Boston is the Phillips Church, which has had a notable succession of pastors, including the late Dr. Alden, the able Secretary of the American Board, Francis Clark, of Endeavor fame, and Dr. R. R. Meredith, of Brooklyn. Its constituency has changed vastly since the days when the section was an aristocratic residential portion, where well-to-do merchants had homes. Yet pressed upon by the incoming tide of foreigners, Phillips Church, having modified its methods, is bravely standing for the faith of the Pilgrims, and under its efficient pastor, Rev. C. A. Dinsmore, is exerting a large influence. It maintains with vigor Phillips Chapel. Similar conditions now prevail at East Boston, where the Maverick Church was for many years one of the pillars of the denomination. It, too, has suffered many reverses, but its spirit is still undismayed, and it has recently called to its leadership Rev. O. D. Fisher. The Baker Church, whose pastor is Rev. J. C. Young, was started three years ago. As we leave East Boston Ferry we ought not to pass by the Seamen's Church, where Capt. S. S. Nickerson keeps open house for the sailors.

At Charlestown we find the oldest Trinitarian Congregational church in the city, the First, dating back to 1632, and having now as its pastor, Rev. C. H. Pope, and the Winthrop, whose pastor is Rev. W. B. Forbush. Both of these churches have played a creditable part in the life of the denomination.

There are only two foreign churches of our order in Boston — the Swedish, which has a home of its own in Roxbury, and the Norwegian, which worships in Shawmut vestry.

The total church membership of the thirty-two Boston churches January 1, 1899, was 11,685; Sunday-school membership, 13,237. The reported benevolences were $94,225.

CITY MISSIONARY WORK

The right hand of the Congregational churches of Boston is the *City Missionary Society*, of which Richard H. Stearns, Esq., is President, and Rev. D. W. Waldron, Superintendent and Secretary. Its widespread work is administered from Room 602 in the Congregational House, 14 Beacon Street.

The Society was founded in 1816, when Boston was a town with less than forty thousand inhabitants. The leaven of active Christian life set at work through this agency transformed what was then the degraded quarter of the city, began the system of primary education, established Sunday-schools, inaugurated work among sailors and other exceptional classes, and aided in founding some of the strongest churches in Boston.

The problems presented for solution have grown with the twelvefold growth of Boston, and the continuous purpose of the Society is to leaven so much of the population as it can reach with the transforming elements of Christian kindness and Christian truth.

During 1898 twenty-three missionaries were employed. The receipts were $47,544.52.

Although figures are inadequate to express spiritual influences or show what has been accomplished in the upbuilding of character, yet when they represent Christian and benevolent work, they have an impressive meaning and importance, and the record, in part, of labors and results for the past year appear in the following tabulated statement: —

Visits made, 62,413; different families visited, 22,794; visits to the sick, 4,368; copies of the Scriptures distributed, 575; papers and tracts distributed, 113,163; meetings held, 2,137; children gathered into Sunday-schools, 816; persons hopefully converted, 64; persons furnished employment, 485; families afforded pecuniary aid, 1,499.

Congregationalism in Greater Boston

Swift and cheap transportation has so knit the cities and towns around Boston to it that of late years the name Metropolitan District has been coined to apply to the region within a ten-mile circuit of the State House, and special boards have been created to have charge of the water supply and to oversee the development of the park system on a similarly broad scale. The religious life and problems before the churches have naturally been affected by this metropolitan expansion and unification, and any large view of Congregational forces in the city ought to include the twenty-eight cities and towns which in many of their interests are practically one with Boston itself. In order to promote a sense of unity between the churches, the Congregational Church Union of Boston and vicinity was formed three years ago, and is doing a valuable and needed work in bringing the aid of the stronger churches to the weaker, in establishing new enterprises in promising sections, and in fostering the growth of the denomination at other points where it has long been established. It has no paid officers, but is efficiently administered by a board of twenty-seven directors. The President is Hon. S. C. Darling, the Secretary, Mr. J. J. Tillinghast, and the Treasurer, Mr. C. E. Kelsey.

Much of the best life of the city churches has gone into the outlying cities and towns, and some of the strongest and most prosperous representatives of the denomination are now to be found in them.

Harvard Church, of Brookline, of which Rev. Reuen Thomas, D.D., well known in England, is pastor, has a splendid equipment and a prestige equaled by few Congregational churches throughout the country. Its echo organ is as pleasing

HARVARD CHURCH, BROOKLINE.

as it is rare. Until the recent formation of Leyden Church in the newer portion of the town, Harvard had been the only representative of our polity in this beautiful and patrician suburb.

Further out, at Newton, we have a circle of six churches, prominent among them being the Eliot, with a fine structure, ample wealth, and a wide influence, Rev. W. H. Davis, D.D., pastor. The First Church, situated at Newton Centre, has also taken its place in the front rank, and its growth compels it to erect soon a new house of worship. Dr. Daniel L. Furber has long been the honored pastor *emeritus*. Rev. E. M. Noyes is pastor.

In Cambridge we have six churches, one of them — the First, or the Shepard Memorial — the mother of all, having Rev. Alexander McKenzie, D.D., as its pastor. Its daughters in other sections of the city show themselves worthy of the parent stock. Certain of the parishes of Cambridge and those of Somerville overlap, but there is a distinct Congregational life and atmosphere in the latter city, and no less than six substantial churches. At Chelsea we have three churches, which hold a leading place in the religious life of the city. Malden and Everett are to be credited with three, and still further to the north, at Lynn, we are represented by five churches.

On the other side of the city, Quincy has shown, of late years, a most remarkable growth Congregationally, having now no less than six churches. In other suburban places, where the denomination is represented by one or two churches only, as in Melrose, Wakefield, Stoneham, Woburn, Winchester, Medford, Arlington, Lexington, Waltham, Watertown, Hyde Park, Milton, and Revere, we find, as a rule, vigor and alertness to opportunity, and many fruitful activities.

ELIOT CHURCH, NEWTON.

OTHER DENOMINATIONS IN BOSTON

Congregationalism in Boston cheerfully accords to its sister denominations, which were all later in the field, the honor which is their due for what they have wrought, and for their present zeal and efficiency. The Baptists in the metropolitan district, from the point of view of membership and benevolence, stand next to the Congregationalists, and much of their work is notable for its evangelistic ardor. Tremont Temple, in the heart of the city, draws its great congregations from perhaps thirty cities and towns, and there is no more impressive and inspiring service on Sunday in the city than either its morning or evening gathering. Rev. George C. Lorimer, D.D., has maintained his vigorous leadership for a number of years, and apparently his grip on the people was never stronger. The Ruggles Street, at Roxbury, deserves special mention because of its institutional character, its great Sunday-school, and its famous quartette, as well as for its numerous week-day ministrations. A similar aggressive work, though on a smaller scale and in behalf of a lower element, is carried on at the Bowdoin Square Tabernacle. The most fashionable Baptist church is that on Commonwealth Avenue, whose pastor, Rev. Nathan E. Wood, D.D., has just been called to the presidency of the Newton Theological Seminary. Clarendon Street is associated with the beloved name of Rev. A. J. Gordon, D.D.

Methodism has two down-town representatives, Bromfield Street and Temple Street, and two at the South End, the People's Temple and Tremont Street, all of which have been the centers of strong spiritual influences and the scene of many revivals, though, like their sister churches of other denominations, they have had to wrestle with the problems peculiar to a great city. Methodism is also fairly well represented in the suburbs. Boston University is a pillar of strength to it.

KING'S CHAPEL.

KING'S CHAPEL, *corner of School and Tremont Streets, built of wood in 1688, rebuilt of stone in 1749-54. The portico was built in 1789 from funds partly raised by an oratorio in the chapel, at which General Washington attended " attired in a black velvet suit, and gave five guineas." The organ, the first used in America, was purchased in England in 1756. During the siege of Boston the British officers worshiped here. The chapel has marble busts of its former pastors,— Freeman, Greenwood, Peabody, and Foote, — and mural monuments of Apthorp, Appleton, Lowell, Oliver Wendell Holmes, and Joseph May.*

Other Denominations in Boston

As respects the Episcopal churches, the stranger would naturally turn first toward Trinity, where Phillips Brooks' silver voice was so long heard as it pealed forth the glad tidings. Since his death the church has not languished, but, on the other hand, continues to be widely popular and at times thronged. Rev. E. W. Donald, D.D., who was born and bred a Congregationalist, has proved no unworthy successor to Bishop Brooks. Another strong Episcopal church on the Back Bay, which by its recent enlargement has obtained one of the most efficient church plants in the city, is the Emmanuel, of which Rev. Leighton Parks, D.D., is pastor. Down town St. Paul's plain gray structure faces busy Tremont Street, while at the West End the church of the Advent stands for the high church element in Episcopacy, and is well attended both by its regular constituency and those who go out of curiosity. Service continues to be held at the old Christ Church at the North End. The Episcopalians support a vigorous city missionary society, which not only relieves the condition of the poor, but oversees the starting and developing of new enterprises, and labors, too, in behalf of seamen.

In some respects, Boston may be regarded as the stronghold of Unitarianism, and they have about sixty churches in the metropolitan district. Dr. Edward Everett Hale has been for many years the foremost member of the denomination, though he has just resigned his charge at the South Church. The Arlington Street Church, fronting the Public Garden, may perhaps be regarded as a typical Unitarian church in the city, and one whose service will repay attendance. King's Chapel possesses more suggestiveness on account of its unique history. Here Dr. Oliver Wendell Holmes worshiped, and the service has a decidedly Episcopalian flavor.

If one is looking up interesting churches of other faiths and orders, he should not pass the Universalist church on Shawmut

Avenue, known as the Every Day Church; or the Christian Science Temple, just off Huntington Avenue, to which at certain seasons of the year, as the mother church, Christian Scientists from all over the country to the number of thousands resort; or the Spiritual Temple on the Back Bay, where on almost any Sunday evening Gladstone, Napoleon, and other notables who have passed into the spiritual world may, as it is alleged, be communicated with. A look at the announcements of Sunday services in the Saturday morning papers will give the visitor some idea of the immense variety and diverse character of religious services held in the city on a single Sunday. Upon the western mall of the Common one finds, on pleasant Sunday afternoons during the summer, a remarkable variety of open air preaching.

Philanthropic work has been carried to a notable degree of perfection. To the Boston City Missionary Society, a Congregational institution, we refer elsewhere. The Associated Charities, more secular in its methods, does much to relieve suffering and poverty. The youth of the city are well provided for through a vigorous Young Men's Christian Association and a Young Men's Christian Union, and the Young Women's Christian Association. The college and social settlement movement has taken a firm root in the city. The South End House, whose residents are men, the Denison House, where women only live, Lincoln House, which has a splendid network of educational agencies, and the Peabody House, where the kindergarten movement is most prominent, are the strongest institutions of the sort, and a visitor will find much to reward his investigations.

Literary and Educational Boston

Not without good reason has Boston long been conceded to be unsurpassed by any other American city as a literary and educational center. And, although its significant buildings or institutions are somewhat scattered, most of them can be visited easily.

In the Congregational House itself, the Congregational Library should be seen. In its beautiful reading room are portraits of departed leaders of our body, and its collection of books, rich in sociological and notably in Pilgrim and colonial literature, daily grows more valuable. Hon. S. B. Pratt's comprehensive Biblearium is remarkable; and the other objects of interest in the cabinet room also deserve attentive study. Our denominational bookstore also is worth a visit. It means much to any branch of the church to have a depot of supplies so well stocked and manned.

Leaving the House and turning down Beacon Street, the very next building arrests one. It is the Boston Athenæum. Here are a valuable library and art gallery, and, although belonging to a private corporation, their treasures are not forbidden to others. President George Washington's private library is a special feature. In the same building is the hall of the American Academy of Arts and Sciences, with a single exception the oldest scientific society in America. It was founded in 1780, always has had a distinguished membership, and has charge of the bestowal of the Rumford medals.

Nearly opposite, Somerset Street enters Beacon. Passing a little way up the former, one reaches the principal buildings of the Boston University. This institution, founded in 1869 by the Methodists, includes several distinct colleges and professional schools, and has obtained a high rank. Rev. W. F.

Warren, D.D., is its head. Its theological department is the oldest and one of the best in the Methodist body, and its schools of law and medicine also are eminent. It modest external appearance affords no adequate suggestion of its actual educational importance. Continuing down Somerset Street from Ashburton Place, it is only a few steps to the home of the New England Historic Genealogical Society, a treasury of antiquarian objects and a center of genealogical research. The organization is large and flourishing, publishes an admirable *Register*, and welcomes and aids the public with frank hospitality.

If one is interested in book shops and publishing houses, he will, when on Washington Street, look in at the bookstore of Messrs. Little, Brown & Co., for their firm long has been a leader in its line. He will also pause at the lower corner of Washington and School Streets to notice the Old Corner Bookstore, now occupied by Messrs. Cupples, Upham & Co. It is one of the oldest edifices in the city, dating from 1712, and for three quarters of a century it has been preëminently the resort of the most eminent authors and their friends. Messrs. N. J. Bartlett & Co., at 28 Cornhill, do a large business with ministers and their store is a clerical rendezvous. They are good Congregationalists, by the way. So are Messrs. T. Y. Crowell & Co., who have their main business in New York, but maintain a considerable establishment not far down town on Purchase Street. The Charles E. Lauriat Co., on Washington Street, makes a specialty of old and rare books. Messrs. Small, Maynard & Co., near the northern end of Beacon Street, are one of the most enterprising of the younger publishing firms.

Where Park Street ascends the gentle slope to the State House is the publishing house of Houghton, Mifflin & Co., which issues *The Atlantic Monthly*, through which Holmes, Longfellow, Lowell, Hawthorne, Emerson, Whipple, Whittier, Thoreau, and other great New England writers of the century

PARK STREET, LOOKING TOWARD THE STATE HOUSE.

MASSACHUSETTS INSTITUTE OF TECHNOLOGY.

now closing used to delight to address their public. It is the State Library which we are chiefly seeking in the State House, which Mr. C. B. Tillinghast, the librarian, makes readily available by all. It is exceptionally rich in statute books, political economy, social science, etc.

A short distance from the State House down Mt. Vernon Street the General Theological Library is to be found, with Rev. G. W. Jackson, a loyal Congregationalist, at its head. It is unsectarian and is much appreciated by the clerical profession.

The New England Magazine, which reproduces so faithfully the different characteristics of New England thought and life, has its office in Park Square.

In the newer portion of the city, only a single block from the Garden, are several stately buildings. The first is that of the Boston Society of Natural History, founded in 1831, in which are valuable mineral and other collections. The society provides lecture courses and publishes works on natural history, and its building is open to the public two days in the week. The two other buildings belong to the Massachusetts Institute of Technology, incorporated in 1861, one of the largest and most justly renowned institutions of its class. Prof. James M. Crafts recently has succeeded the late Gen. Francis A. Walker as its president.

Continuing still westward through Copley Square, the Girls' Latin School is passed on one's right about at the middle of the block, and on the other side of the street, a little further out, stands the Harvard Medical School, a department of Harvard University. The Warren Anatomical Museum, the gift of Dr. John Collins Warren, is a special feature. It adjoins the Boston Public Library, described in a previous article, and notable for its departments of newspapers, photographs, etc., and its special libraries, of colonial and theological works, of music, etc. The fine new edifice of the Massachusetts His-

ROXBURY LATIN SCHOOL.

Literary and Educational Boston

torical Society, the oldest organization of its kind in America, stands some ten minutes' walk further west at the corner of Boylston Road and the Fenway. It has a library and museum, each rich in rare treasures.

On Dartmouth Street, a few blocks eastward from Copley Square, is the Normal School, devoted to training school teachers. It is conceded to be much above the average in efficiency. Not far away, too, are the English High School for boys on Montgomery Street, that for girls on West Newton Street, and the Boys' Latin School on Warren Avenue. Each is a source of just pride to all Bostonians, and the visitor will be welcomed should he desire to enter either or all.

The musical visitor also will like to inspect the New England Conservatory of Music. To reach it he must pass eastward to Washington Street, one of the great thoroughfares of the city, and then must follow that street westward as far as the two opposite squares, Franklin and Blackstone. The Conservatory is the principal object in sight on the west side of the former. It is practically the monument of its indefatigable founder, the late Dr. Eben Tourjée, who established it in 1867. It affords a thorough and comprehensive musical education at a comparatively low cost.

Only ten years younger than the historic Boston Latin School is the Roxbury Latin School, formerly known as "The Grammar School in the easterly part of the Town of Roxbury." It was founded in 1645, by John Eliot and Gov. Thomas Dudley, and among its teachers before the Revolution were Judge William Cushing, Gen. Joseph Warren, and Gov. Increase Sumner. In later years the list of instructors and pupils contains many well-known names. Its building is a large wooden structure on Kearsarge Avenue.

Short Trips around Boston

Few cities in the world have more attractive suburbs than has Boston, and no city in the United States has a public park system at all comparable with that of the city of Boston and those controlled by the Metropolitan Park Commission. Add to these beautiful natural resorts the many houses and monuments of historical or literary interest scattered about in the towns and cities of the metropolitan area, and the sight-seer from abroad has no difficulty in spending his moments spared from business or conference on spiritual themes in ways that are both pleasing and informing. Nor is it difficult to journey about the city and its suburbs, thanks to the splendid service of the great electric surface railway system, whose tracks thread the streets of Greater Boston and carry passengers swiftly and cheaply to their destinations, furnishing transfers as often as occasion demands.

Of the city parks those best worth visiting are,

The Common, in the heart of the city, with St. Gaudens' Monument to Robert G. Shaw.

The Public Garden, adjacent to the Common, with statues of Sumner, Everett, and Washington.

The Charlesbank (take electrics at Bowdoin Square or Park Square), notable for its playgrounds and baths for the poor.

Jamaica Park (take electrics at Union Station, North, or Park Street Subway), on the banks of Jamaica Pond, and including the estate formerly owned by Parkman, the historian.

Franklin Park (take electrics at Park Street Subway, Union Stations), named after Benjamin Franklin, largest in area, with fine views of the Blue Hills of Milton, which are also in a reservation controlled by the Metropolitan Park Commission, and are the highest land in Eastern Massachusetts.

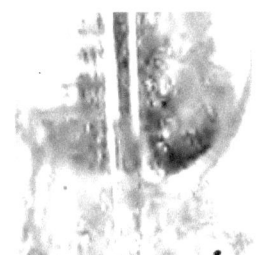

Short Trips around Boston

Marine Park, South Boston Point (take electrics at Union Stations, or Park Square and Charles Street), gives fine view of harbor, cool breezes, etc.

Of the parks under the care of the Metropolitan Park Commission, those best worth visiting are : —

Middlesex Fells (take electrics for Medford, at Scollay Square or Union Station, North), a wild, wooded tract of rare beauty and in a virgin state. Adjoining these on the north and east are the Lynn Woods, a similar tract, accessible from Lynn, which is reached by electrics from Scollay Square or by train on the Boston & Maine Railroad.

Revere Beach (take Lynn and Boston electrics, Scollay Square and Union Station, North, or Lynn and Revere Beach Railroad, Atlantic Avenue), with its fine view on the North Atlantic ocean and its admirable public bath house, interesting as a new development of state activity in Massachusetts.

Waverley Oaks and Beaver Brook (take electrics for Waverley at Park Street Subway Station), finest oak timber in the country, and a scene haunted by James Russell Lowell and frequently referred to by him in his verse.

To those interested in arboriculture, horticulture, and the like, the Arnold Arboretum (take Forest Hills electrics at Union Stations, Scollay Square, or Park Street), owned by Harvard University, the largest and finest tree museum in the world, and the Botanical Gardens, Cambridge (take Huron Avenue, Cambridge electrics, and get off at Bond Street), are well worth visiting, especially the former.

By water one can sail to Nantasket or Nahant, the former trip giving one an interesting survey of the beauties of the harbor of Boston and its fortifications, and a glimpse of a popular seaside resort, the latter revealing the beauties of one of the oldest and still most popular resorts on the north shore, chiefly owned and inhabited by the wealthier residents of

PRESENT BUILDINGS AT BROOK FARM, WEST ROXBURY.

Boston, and formerly the summer home of Longfellow and site of the working laboratory of Louis Agassiz. The sail to Gloucester or Salem Willows from Boston is rewarding to those who can spare the time. Boats on all these lines depart from wharves along Atlantic Avenue. See time-tables in local press.

To see the homes of the well-to-do and the wealthier elements of the population, Roxbury and Dorchester on the south, Brookline and Newton on the southwest and west, and Cambridge and Arlington on the west and northwest, may be inspected, either by carriage or in the electrics. West Roxbury (take Forest Hills electrics at Park Street or the steam cars at Park Square) is notable as the scene of Theodore Parker's early labors, and as the town in which the Brook Farm experiment in communism was tried. From Mt. Bellevue, a hill in this suburb, a superb view of harbor, city, and the country inland is to be had.

Ancient Charlestown is near the heart of the city, and can soon be reached by electrics from Park Street and Scollay Square. Its chief interest to the visitor now is in the Bunker Hill Monument, marking the site of the Anglo-American battle of Breed's Hill, June 16, 17, 1775; in the grave of Rev. John Harvard, founder of Harvard College; and in the United States Navy Yard, with its barracks, dry dock, arsenal, etc. S. F. B. Morse, inventor of the electric telegraph and son of a Congregational clergyman, was born in this city.

Visitors interested in problems of municipal administration will profit by inspection of the metropolitan park, sewer, and water systems, by which Greater Boston is given a unified service at low cost. Information concerning the park service may be obtained at the commission's headquarters in the Congregational House, 14 Beacon Street; concerning the water service at No. 3 Mt. Vernon Street; and concerning the sewerage service at No. 1 Mt. Vernon Street.

The Pilgrim Sight-seer in Newe Towne
(Cambridge and Newton)

The well-informed, wide-visioned Congregationalist, whether English or American, who comes to Boston and vicinity for a tour of exploration, is irresistibly and speedily drawn across the Charles River to the city of Cambridge, which is within the confines of that township which Thomas Dudley and Simon Bradstreet established in 1631 and called The Newe Towne. The pilgrim's interest in the place may arise both from what the city has been, and from what it now is. If for the latter reason, he must reckon with its great University (Harvard), its college for women (Radcliffe), its three divinity schools, its large number of book-making establishments (the Riverside Press, the University Press, Ginn & Co., etc.), its exemption from saloons, although a city of more than eighty thousand inhabitants, this exemption having become a fixed municipal policy, and its stable administration of city affairs on a non-partisan basis. Nor can he fail to enjoy the picturesqueness of the landscape as he studies the hills of Brookline and Brighton, looking out across the aforetime meadows of the Charles. Neither can he successfully resist the impression of antiquity and dignified comfort and ease which descends on him as he rambles about the campus of the ancient university, or up and down the streets of Old Cambridge, or saunters out Brattle Street way to Elmwood, the home of Lowell.

But unless one is especially interested in some aspect of modern education or municipal administration, or is a devout enough admirer of William James, John Fiske, Charles Eliot Norton, or T. W. Higginson to make him anxious to hunt out their homes,— which he might well do,— his interest in the city will center chiefly in the haunts of those men of the past who,

From Guide to Metropolitan Boston
Copyright, 1899, Geo. H. Walker & Co.

SHEPARD CHURCH, CAMBRIDGE.

whether as ecclesiastics, teachers, scientists, historians, poets, or publicists, have made Harvard and Cambridge world-famed.

Those, for instance, who know Thomas Hooker's exalted place in the history of constitution-making for English-speaking peoples will reverently seek out that one of the University buildings (Boylston Hall) which now stands on the site of the homestead occupied by him when he, the Cambridge graduate, was pastor of the little flock at Newtowne, 1633-36.

Others will wish to resurrect with the eye of the imagination the primitive conditions which prevailed in and around what is now Harvard Square, when the Puritan divines from throughout the colony came up to Cambridge in 1646-48, and, after prolonged disputation, formulated the Cambridge platform of 1648, "the most important monument of early New England Congregationalism."

Passing out from Harvard Square to the northwest, one passes the edifice of the First Parish Church (Unitarian), then the ancient burying ground, then venerable Christ Church (Protestant Episcopal), then Radcliffe College, and soon comes to the edifice of the Shepard Memorial Church, the home of the spiritual descendants of the flock that Thomas Shepard gathered about him after Hooker had left for Connecticut. Space fails here to tell of all that this Oxford graduate did in shaping the history of the Puritan colony, in helping to found Harvard, and in writing polemical and mystical tracts and books, that are studied even to this day by men like Rev. Dr. Alexander Whyte of Edinburgh, who relish the flavor of the old Puritan style, and Shepard's insight into spiritual things. For more than thirty years this church has had as its pastor Rev. Alexander McKenzie, one of the great preachers of the denomination and the land.

Coming down to a later period in national and denominational history, one finds much in Cambridge to remind him of the denominational, internecine strife, commonly known as the Trinitarian-Unitarian controversy. On Divinity Avenue stands the Harvard Divinity School, now undenominational, but during most of its history under control of the Unitarians. From its quiet halls have gone forth men like Jared Sparks, William Henry Channing, Frederick H. Hedge, Theodore Parker, T. W. Higginson, Samuel Longfellow, C. A. Bartol, and F. D. Huntington, and on its teaching staff it has had men like Channing, Hedge, Abbot, and J. H. Thayer. Here it was that R. W. Emerson, in 1858, delivered his iconoclastic epoch-marking address, and from hence have gone forth intellectual influences which have been stimulating to the thought of the whole catholic church, even if at times couched in terms that seemed to be, or that were, destructive of cherished historic dogmas. No man, however hostile he may be to the negations of Unitarianism, can fail to respect the high standard of character and intellect which the students and instructors of this venerable school have shown; and to all who have profited by contact with the literature — homiletical or otherwise — which men like Channing, Parker, Emerson, and Higginson have produced, a visit to the Divinity Hall will be an act of duty.

While there it will be convenient to visit the admirable Semitic Museum of Harvard University, sheltered in a building adjacent to the Divinity School and cared for by Prof. D. G. Lyon of the Divinity School. This collection is proving of greatest practical value, not only to the teachers and students of the theological seminaries in Cambridge, but to all Bible students in Greater Boston, who are finding out that Professor Lyon and his assistants are most happy to make the collections serviceable and helpful to all who apply.

To the lover of literature and science, Cambridge has peculiar attractions. Here Louis Agassiz and Asa Gray labored and won immortality by their varied contributions to zoölogy,

LONGFELLOW'S HOME.

botany, and biology. The vast Agassiz Museum is the noble monument of the former. The botanical gardens and laboratories of the University are still tokens of the inspiring example of the latter. The simple Christian faith of both of these men is a cherished memory in Cambridge. They never lost their heads, and thus their faith, when the new vistas opened up by the hypothesis of evolution was broached, stretched out before them; and it is gratifying to residents of Cambridge now that they have as a fellow citizen Mr. John Fiske, whose writings, as an interpreter of theistic evolution and as a reconciler of religion and science, equal in lucidity and depth his writings on American history.

Cambridge is the birthplace of Oliver Wendell Holmes, James Russell Lowell, and T. W. Higginson, and the long-time home of Henry Wadsworth Longfellow. All four are inseparably associated with the history of the town, and all of them have embalmed in prose and verse their impressions and reminiscences of Cambridge life. The homes of Longfellow and Lowell are still in the possession of their kindred and are carefully cared for. The parsonage in which Dr. Holmes was born has been destroyed, but its site is marked by a tablet, standing in front of Austin Hall, the Harvard Law School.

Cambridge at different times has been the home of men and women distinguished in many walks of life, — such persons as Richard Henry Dana, Margaret Fuller, C. P. Cranch, W. D. Howells, Arthur Hugh Clough, — and it always has in its floating population a considerable number of *literati*, attracted by its libraries, its lectures, and its society.

For those who crave the privilege of standing by the graveside of the famous dead, Cambridge offers an opportunity unparalleled in America. In Mt. Auburn Cemetery repose Lowell, Longfellow, Holmes, Agassiz, W. H. Prescott, Francis Parkman, Phillips Brooks, Charles Sumner, Edward Everett,

The Pilgrim Sight-seer in Newe Towne

Rufus Choate, Edwin Booth, and Charlotte Cushman — to mention only a few of the better known among its distinguished dead.

But after all that is historical and literary in its associations in Cambridge is seen, the resident or the visitor is forced to admit that the dominating factor in the city's life is the oldest and largest of our American universities. From its inception in 1636 to the present day Harvard has profoundly affected the political, intellectual, and religious life of the American people. Tribunes of the people like Samuel Adams, Wendell Phillips, and Charles Sumner, administrators like the Adamses and Leonard Wood, poets like Lowell, Emerson, and Holmes, jurists like Joseph Story, Horace Gray, and Joseph Choate, divines like Channing and Brooks, historians like Bancroft, Prescott, Parkman, and Motley, and educators like Eliot, have come forth from her loins. Without aid from the State, save in the earliest days of her life, she has acquired property from private donors, which, with revenue derived from tuition fees, gives her an annual income of more than a million dollars a year. The feeble college of the seventeenth century has become a university with ten departments, employing 411 professors and instructors, and ministering to the desires of 4,660 students, including those registered in its summer school.

The ancient buildings, such as Massachusetts, Harvard, Holworthy, and Hollis, still stand about the beautiful quadrangle, memorials of a type of architecture which has enough merit to have survived a temporary eclipse and has emerged in some of the later buildings constructed by the university, such as the Perkins and Conant dormitories and the Phillips Brooks Memorial building, which will be dedicated in the fall. Gore Hall, the home of the splendid library — the third largest in the United States and surpassed by none in the variety and richness of its collections — is modeled after the Gothic build-

HARVARD COLLEGE GATEWAY.

MASSACHUSETTS HALL. — MEMORIAL HALL. — GORE HALL.

ings of the English universities. Memorial Hall, largest and most imposing of all the university's buildings, is the noble monument erected in honor of the ninety-five Harvard students who gave their lives in the Civil War. Its interior beauty, architecturally speaking, and its many splendid decorations — portraits, busts, stained glass windows and the like — give it an interest all its own. Sever Hall and Austin Hall are worth study as specimens of the work of one of the most promising of American architects, H. H. Richardson, who designed Trinity Church, Boston, and whose premature death was a sad loss to the cause of æsthetics in the United States.

Crossing the Charles River just above where it flows near Mt. Auburn, and journeying southward, one soon comes to the present city of Newton, and within its borders he finds a striking display of suburban comfort and beauty. But to the Congregational pilgrim the town derives its chief glory from the fact that near Nonantum Hill John Eliot, the Puritan apostle to the Indians, carried on his work of evangelization — a work that not only included preaching and oral teaching, but also the scholarly task of translating the Bible into the native tongue. This work appealed strongly not only to the sympathy of the Christian congregation established in the colony, but also to the generosity of the Puritan congregations in England, Parliament authorizing the incorporation of a society especially established to promote and propagate the Gospel among the Indians. John Eliot, a graduate of Jesus College, Cambridge University, England, was the first Congregational home missionary in America, a prototype of a noble army of men and women who since his day have been the salt which has kept sweet the life of pioneer settlements, as ever westward empire has taken its irresistible way.

The Pilgrim Sight-Seer in Salem

Congregationalists ought to have a special interest in Salem. Here the first church of their order in the New World was formed. Here the building is still preserved in which those pioneers in adventure and faith worshiped. Here the original ecclesiastical pattern has been many times duplicated.

The present city — the second chartered in the State — although now numbering only some 35,000 inhabitants, lives on something beside its memories.

As the visitor by train steps forth upon Washington Street, he looks through a railway tunnel, which pierces the ridge, separating the north and south rivers. Along this, were scattered the cabins of the first settlers. Essex Street, the chief business thoroughfare, follows in the main the primitive village path. This is crossed by Washington Street, at what was then and still is the center of the place, and is known as Town House Square. Here electric cars may be taken for North and South Salem, Marblehead, Danvers, Peabody, Beverly, and "The Willows," a popular seashore resort. Just beyond the depot, on the right, Central Street leads directly into Charter. Entering this, as the monument to "Father Mathew" is passed, one comes to the large three-story wooden house where Nathaniel Hawthorne found his wife, Miss Sophia Peabody. The novelist has associated this building with the story of "Dr. Grimshawe's Secret." It adjoins the oldest cemetery in the city, then called "Burying Point." Here are the tombs of Bradstreet, the second governor, John Higginson, minister of the First Church, and of a precocious younger brother of Cotton Mather, who died "an aged man at nineteen years," and the ancestors of many prominent families in New England.

Proceeding along Charter Street, the Salem Hospital, a well-

GENERAL VIEW OF SALEM.

endowed charity, is passed and the large church of the Immaculate Conception, when at a turn in the road, Derby Street is reached. Bordering this once busy highway were the stately dwellings of ship owners and masters of vessels, their warehouses and offices; while at the extended wharves lay the fleet of merchant ships, which made the name of Salem even better known than that of Massachusetts or the United States, in many Oriental countries. The inscription on the city seal — "*Divitis Indiæ usque ad ultimum sinum,*" "To the farthest port of the rich East" — was once much more pertinent than now. These residences, with the decline of foreign commerce, have fallen into neglect and decay, and become, in the main, tenement houses, dreary in contrast with their former dignity. On Union Street, a few steps to the right bring one to the birthplace of Hawthorne, that most eminent, brilliant, moody, misunderstood of all her sons, whose fame attracts multitudes to the city.

On Derby Street again, the visitor cannot but note the many gambrel-roofed houses; the Home for Aged Women; the Custom House, chiefly interesting because Hawthorne, while collector of the port, was said to have found there the "scarlet letter," which suggested the title for his most familiar romance. Coming to Turner Street, the tourist asks for and is shown the "House of Seven Gables" (so called), though the author of the story distinctly affirms he had no particular house in mind during the writing. At this point is a charming view of the harbor and of the Marblehead shore. Here, too, the Marine Society's Bethel floats and rings its invitation to the sailor to worship in a tasteful sanctuary.

Returning and crossing Derby, we come to the lower part of Essex Street, and see on the right the Bentley School for Girls. The bell in the tower — cast by Paul Revere — once hung in the steeple of the East Unitarian Church, while the rooster

CUSTOM HOUSE AND POST OFFICE, SALEM.

which perches above it lifted his head at the top of the old church spire. Dr. William Bentley, the pastor, was among the earliest and most able of the Unitarian leaders in this country, having unusual antiquarian and scientific gifts.

On the right, Pleasant Street leads to the largest park in the city, called after the President, "Washington Square." About it are grouped substantial homes, many dating from the early days of the present century. Not a few present the best styles of colonial architecture and many elaborate doorways and porches.

At Winter Street, in the first brick dwelling on the left, Judge Joseph Story lived. There his son, the poet and sculptor, W. W. Story, was born. Returning to the Square, the plain mansion of the late George Peabody, nephew of the London philanthropist, attracts attention. It is among the best of our colonial edifices, and is now in the possession of the Salem Club.

On Mall Street, at No. 14, was the study where Hawthorne wrote "The Snow Image" and "The Scarlet Letter." There are many pilgrimages to the scene of that matchless creation.

In the Brown Street court, near by, stands the quaint house where Nathaniel Bowditch, the learned mathematician and translator of the "Principia" and the "Mécanique Céleste," was born, as also the Rev. Samuel Johnson, the eminent scholar and author of "Oriental Religions."

Passing to Essex Street, our course is to the right and to the Essex Institute building, the archæological center of the city. Within its walls is gathered a unique collection of relics. Articles illustrating every phase of the social, political, literary, artistic, business life and history of the town and county are here displayed.

Adjoining it is the Salem Athenæum, a corporation library of some 22,000 volumes, with an appropriate hall where lec-

The Pilgrim Sight-seer in Salem

tures and concerts and art and horticultural exhibitions are given. Here distinguished travelers and visitors from our own and foreign lands have been received and addressed appreciative audiences. The building stands upon the site of one in which Prescott, the historian, was born.

In the rear is the frame of the first Protestant church built in America, in 1634. Its covering is of course modern, but the restoration to the original is as nearly perfect as the imagination can make it. Within the little audience room, beneath the diminutive gallery, are to be seen valuable reminders of the days of yore. A keen ear may possibly detect there still the mellow tones of the godly Higginson, and the more emphatic sounds with which Williams kept the drowsy worshipers awake.

Next the Athenæum is the headquarters of the Second Corps Cadets. The house abounds in choice carving in wood and marble, while the banquet hall, finished in oak after the style of the Elizabethan period, and with stained windows and figures of kings and queens and men-at-arms, is unsurpassed by any, at least in this section of the land. Here Prince Arthur of England was entertained.

On Essex Street again, we come to the Peabody Institute, named for George Peabody, who gave $140,000 to further the work in which its trustees were engaged. The East India Marine Society's Museum was secured, and its rare treasures, brought from all parts of the world, were merged in the larger purpose than that of mere curiosity, namely, of scientific study. One might profitably spend days in looking through its carefully arranged and constantly increasing cabinets. In the lecture hall, Story's beautiful statue of "Medea" graces the platform.

Take St. Peter Street and stop a moment at St. Peter's Episcopal Church, a mediæval stone structure, though erected in

FIRST CHURCH, SALEM.

1833. In the tower is a chime of ten bells, the oldest cast in England, in 1740.

Passing the Central Baptist Church and the "Ward House," with its projecting second story, the County Jail will be interesting to Congregationalists, as having been for thirty days the prison of Dr. George B. Cheever, then pastor of Howard Street Church, for alleged criminal libel through the publication, in a local paper, of an article, "Deacon Giles' Distillery." This was soon printed and distributed as a temperance tract.

A short walk and Washington Street is again reached, on the corner of which is the Tabernacle Church. It dates — by courtesy, and for peace's sake — from 1735, though a very satisfactory argument can be made showing its right to be recognized as the *original* First Church. In this right the South Congregational Church claims an equal share. In the building standing on the site of the present meeting-house, the first foreign missionaries, Newell, Judson, Nott, Hall, and Rice, were ordained, February 6, 1812, during the pastorate of Dr. Samuel Worcester, first secretary of the American Board. The settee used on that occasion is preserved in the church parlors. The present pastor is Rev. DeWitt S. Clark, D.D.

In the clerk's office of the Court House, succeeding the first, which stood near the middle of Washington Street, are carefully kept the records of the witchcraft trials; the warrant for the execution of Bridget Bishop duly returned by the sheriff, and a bottle containing some of the pins produced during the trials, as having been thrust into their victims by the accused.

Resuming the pilgrimage on "Federal Street," and passing the First Baptist Church, turning at North Street and crossing the railway, one comes to the "North Bridge."

It is a revelation to many, that here the first armed resistance to the royal authority was made, February 26, 1775, two

months before the Lexington fight. English visitors will look upon this spot with even greater satisfaction than Bunker Hill, for here no English blood was shed, — the American power of persuasion through the lips of brave Parson Barnard, who had hurriedly dismissed his congregation that Sunday to protect the " munitions " of the colonists, being mightier than Colonel Leslie's bayonets. This is recounted on a bronze tablet in the massive stone monument at the bridge.

Returning past the Wesley Church, we come to the oldest house in the city, built in 1634, and known as the " Old Witch House," since Judge Corwin, before whom some of the preliminary examinations of the suspects were made, lived here. It should be called, the rather, the " Roger Williams' House," as he built and resided in it while minister of the First Church, and went forth from it into banishment, because of his practical exposition of the doctrine of " Soul Liberty." The North Unitarian Church, and its ample yard with its wide-branching elms, is without question the most picturesque of all our religious edifices. A little distance beyond is the colonial house, until recently occupied by Judge William C. Endicott, Secretary of War under President Cleveland, and whose daughter is the wife of Right Hon. Joseph Chamberlain, of England.

Nearly opposite is the Public Library of more than 34,000 volumes. Pilgrims to Gallows Hill would do well to take the electrics here, and, leaving at Hanson Street, climb a steep ascent to a barren, wind-swept plateau where, 207 years ago, nineteen victims of the dreadful witchcraft delusion were hanged on locust trees, no trace of which can now be found. Nor is there monument or sign to mark the precise spot. The present generation would be only too glad to obliterate all that fearful record, but no martyrs for the truth ever died more grandly. None deserve a better memorial.

The stranger should not fail to stroll through Chestnut

GALLOWS HILL. SALEM. OLD SHATTUCK HOUSE.

WITCH HOUSE, SALEM.

The Pilgrim Sight-seer in Salem

Street, whose elegant homes give a hint of the wealth and taste within, and come to Cambridge Street.

At the corner the South Congregational Church lifts its much-admired spire high above the city roofs. It is the oldest church building now in use, having been erected in 1804, and has been carefully preserved. The interior is handsomely decorated. A beautiful crystal chandelier, imported in the beginning of the century, lights the auditorium. Rev. James F. Brodie is the pastor.

Leaving Chestnut Street at Norman, and turning into Crombie Street, the third of our Congregational churches comes into view. It is under the pastoral care of Rev. John W. Buckham. The church, which was in large degree an offshoot of the Howard Street Church, had among its first trustees Rufus Choate, and has always had influential and cultured families in its congregation. It was formed in 1832, and its list of pastors has been a *starred* one.

One should look in at "Ames Memorial Hall," in the new Young Men's Christian Association building, on Essex Street, the whole edifice being a worthy testimony to the religious and philanthropic spirit of the modern city, and then hasten on to Town House Square. Here was the site of the old Town House where Governor Burnet convened the General Court in 1728; where the House of Assembly, with closed doors, defied General Gage in 1774; and where, the same year, the First Provincial Congress met. Here swung the handle of the old "Town Pump," whose "Rills" Hawthorne has immortalized. Here Endicott daringly cut the cross — the Popish symbol — out of the colors of the Train Bands. Here was the site of the First Church, upon which the present building of that name stands, a brick structure, with stores and banks occupying the lower floor. On its walls is inscribed the solemn league of the founders, beginning, "We covenant with the Lord and

WARD AND CROWNINGSHIELD HOUSE, SALEM.

CABOT AND ENDICOTT HOUSE, SALEM.

one with another." Near by were the houses of the first planters, Conant and Woodbury, coming hither in 1626, of Endicott, the governor, and Hugh Peters and Higginson, pastors of the First Church.

The present City Hall, which has supplanted the ancient Town House, is but a step away, and contains, among many valuable paintings, a faded parchment, on which is engrossed a warranty deed of all the lands in the town, from the heirs of Nanepashemet to the selectmen of Salem in trust for the people. On this, the sons of the forest made each their *peaceful* mark and passed on forever.

As the visitor goes down the same slope, it is to bid farewell to Old "Naumkeag" — the home of the painted Indian — to Salem, the refuge of the persecuted Puritan, the theater of a fatal superstition, the seat of a world-wide enterprise, the scene of valiant witnessing for liberty, the fountain of benevolent Christian impulse, the abode of generous and intelligent appreciation of the best things in life and society — of Salem, a city of the past, the present, and the future; of which all who have been born within her borders are proud, and from which none should depart with less enthusiasm than he brings.

The Pilgrim Sight-Seer in Plymouth.

THAN Old Plymouth on a bright summer day a fairer town cannot easily be found. With the look of thrift and comfort, yet with little of the bustle of a great city, with a pleasantly diversified surface, with its atmosphere tinctured by the tonic fragrance of the neighboring pine forests or by the cool salt breeze blowing in from the sea, with a beautiful outlook over a curving coast-line, an irregular harbor and a wide sweep of open sea, and enriched by many a spot within it forever sacred to the lover of truth and country, it is a place which the visitor learns to enjoy and regrets the more to leave the longer he has remained. Its places of special historic interest are so near each other that one can see them all in a short time.

Assuming that he enters Plymouth by train, he will find himself close to the water front, which for some miles he has been following, with charming views, on his left, of the Bay, Duxbury, Clark's Island, the Gurnet, and the long spur inclosing the southern portion of the harbor and known as Plymouth Beach. Electric cars await him near at hand. But it will be as well for him to turn his steps first towards the National Monument, perhaps half a mile away and not accessible by cars.

Passing up to the main street, and turning to the right in front of the two spacious and comfortable hotels, The Samoset and The Elms, he may take either of the next one or two streets to the left, and an ascent of a few minutes will bring him within sight of a park, in the center of which stands the

The Pilgrim Sight-seer in Plymouth

conspicuous memorial known as the National Monument. Sometimes it is called the Faith Monument. The corner-stone was laid on August 2, 1859. The pedestal is forty-five feet high, and the statue of Faith, which surmounts it, is thirty-six feet. The statue was the gift of the late Hon. Oliver Ames, of Easton, Mass., a native of Plymouth. On each corner buttress of the pedestal is a seated statue, of smaller, yet heroic, size. That representing Morality was given by the State of Massachusetts, and the bas-relief in front of it, depicting The Embarking at Delfshaven, was given by the State of Connecticut. The statue of Education was the gift of Hon. Roland Mather, of Hartford, Conn., together with its bas-relief, Signing the Compact. The other two statues represent Liberty and Law, the former having been erected by the United States Government. The remaining two bas-reliefs represent The Landing of the Pilgrims and The First Treaty with the Indians.

Most of the historic interest of the town, however, is associated with its more central part. Descending the hill again to the main street and turning to the right, one reaches, in only two or three minutes from the hotels, a sort of temple with the roof of its porch upheld by columns, above which, under the peak of the roof, is a bas-relief, representing the Pilgrims landing upon the famous rock. Of course it is purely an imaginary scene and the artist's conception is historically inexact, since he has introduced into his group an Indian, in spite of the fact that they saw no Indians in the vicinity for some weeks after their landing.

This building is the Pilgrim Museum. It is a precious treasury of documents, books, pictures, furniture, weapons, etc., related more or less closely to the first settlers and their life. Its courteous custodians know well how to facilitate the researches of the visitor, but most of its contents are self-

MILES STANDISH'S SWORD, PLATTER, AND KETTLE.

ELDER BREWSTER'S CHAIR. PEREGRINE WHITE'S CRADLE.

The Pilgrim Sight-seer in Plymouth

explanatory. Among the objects of interest are a sword, a pot, and a platter of Miles Standish, chairs of Elder Brewster and Governor Carver, Peregrine White's cradle, John Alden's Bible, portraits in oil of Edward Winslow and his son and others, several important commissions and other documents, and various specimens of old armor, furniture, several of Brewster's books, and other relics. There also are many interesting pictures, including three large paintings, two of which, one by Sargent and one by Lucy, respectively represent the Embarkation of the Pilgrims and the other their Landing at Plymouth. A long time may be spent profitably in examining the collection.

From the Museum it is easiest to go next to the Court House. Continuing towards the south along the main street, one soon comes to a little square on his right hand, facing the upper side of which stands the building sought. On its front is a white marble tablet bearing the seal of the Old Colony. There is nothing specially notable within the building, excepting many old deeds in the Registry Office and the original patent granted to the company in 1629 by the Earl of Warwick. A copy of Miles Standish's will also can be seen.

On leaving the Court House, a short street out of the square on the right leads one soon by a gradual ascent to the northern end of Burial Hill, a low elevation — it is only 165 feet above the sea level — surmounted by tombstones. It is easy of access, and from its level summit there is a fine outlook over the town and the bay. For generations this burying ground served the needs of the colony, and the ancestors of many historic families of our country repose beneath its turf. But it was not their earliest place of burial. For a number of years they laid their dead to rest either on Cole's Hill, near their landing place, or in their private grounds. The oldest gravestone now standing is that of Edward Gray, and is dated 1681.

The Pilgrim Sight-seer in Plymouth

But from a very early period the hill served as a place of defense. In the summer of 1623 they built upon it a fort, a solidly constructed log house of considerable size, quite strong enough to defend its garrison from arrows, the only weapons of the natives, and having a flat roof and battlements on which they mounted their six little cannon and kept a constant watch. Here they also held worship until the erection of the first church building in 1637-38. In 1643 a watchhouse was built near by, as a precaution against the Dutch and the Narragansett Indians. This watchhouse had a brick foundation. Tablets now indicate the sites of both structures. The grave of Gov. William Bradford is close at hand, indicated by a marble obelisk. Those of Robert and Thomas Cushman are near by. Descending the hill by its southeasterly slope, and passing between the Congregational church on the left and the new Unitarian church on the right, one may be sure that he stands in the immediate vicinity of the first church building. The former of the two modern churches is thought to occupy substantially its site. Before him Leyden Street, the earliest street in the town, runs down towards the water. Erase from the landscape in fancy for the moment the modern buildings and replace them by the thatch-roofed log houses of the Pilgrims, and you can seem to see, as you glance down the rude roadway, on your right hand the dwellings and gardens of Edward Winslow, Francis Cooke, Isaac Allerton, John Billington, William Brewster, John Goodman, and Peter Brown, and on your left hand, about halfway down, that of Gov. William Bradford, with those of Stephen Hopkins, John Howland, and Dr. Samuel Fuller below it. At first, in order to economize labor and room, more than one family occupied each house.

Then walk slowly down the street, catching occasional glimpses of the Town Brook through the openings on your right. For years Leyden Street was the chief, if not the only,

NORTH STREET, LOOKING TOWARDS THE BAY, PLYMOUTH.

THE DOTEN HOUSE, 1660.

highway, and it has witnessed many an impressive scene — the entry of Indian embassies, the welcome of newly arrived voyagers from home, the hasty mustering of the colonists for defense or the processions to their little fortress-church for Sabbath worship. At the bottom of the street on the right stood the Common House, first built of all. At present an inscription on a modern house marks the spot. And, as one then turns slightly to the left, he reaches the brow of the little bluff, known as Cole's Hill, where at first the dead were buried, and where, during their terrible first winter, when cold and famine actually carried off one out of every two of the company, the feeble survivors leveled the graves of their loved ones, lest some Indian spy should count the graves.

From Cole's Hill one looks down directly upon the famous Plymouth Rock under its modern canopy of stone. Originally at the water's edge, the rock now lies partially imbedded in the ground, a few score feet from the water. Its canopy consists of four massive pillars supporting a chamber with an arched roof, in which have been deposited bones dug up on Cole's Hill. The canopy is fifteen feet square on the ground and thirty feet high. The rock itself is a granite bowlder.

One may return to Boston by train, or, as many prefer, by steamer, which leaves a pier adjacent to the rock. If the latter alternative be chosen, he passes very near to Clark's Island, on the left as the steamer leaves the inner harbor. There the exploring party spent Sunday, the day before landing on the mainland. Near the middle of it is a large bowlder, under the lee of which, according to a groundless tradition, which nevertheless embodies a possibility, they held their worship. It now is called Pulpit Rock and bears this inscription, "On the Sabboth Day Wee Rested."

PLYMOUTH, FROM ACROSS THE TOWN BROOK.

THE ELM WALK, SEMINARY HILL, ANDOVER.

THE PILGRIM SIGHT-SEER IN ANDOVER

Phillips Brooks, Bishop of Massachusetts in one church, honored, loved, and lamented in all other churches as well, proud of his own descent from an ancient Puritan family of Andover, once said : " If I wanted to give a foreigner some clear idea of what that excellent institution, a New England town, really is, in its history and its character, in its enterprise and its sobriety, in its godliness and its manliness, I should be sure that I could do it if I could make him perfectly familiar with the past and present of Andover." Although the pilgrims who come from Old England to New England on the high errand of Christian communion and conference are indeed no more strangers and foreigners, but fellow citizens with those that welcome them, they may be glad to learn a few facts about this early town of the Massachusetts Bay Colony, thus claimed as typical of the true New England, and which certainly has had, from the first, special bonds of connection with Old England, " mother of us all."

The founders of Andover were all born and reared in England, coming here after a few years' sojourn in earlier settlements on the coast. When the Indian sagamore in 1646 sold " Cochickawick " to Mr. Woodbridge, the first minister, son of a non-conformist clergyman in Wiltshire ("for ye sume of 6£ and a coate "), the name was changed to Andover, in memory of the town in Hants, from which some of the settlers had come. At the 250th celebration in 1896, greetings were received from the town on the Ande, where in a recent visit Principal Bancroft found some of the ancient family names of our American town.

A reference to one of the founders must suffice for all. Simon

The Pilgrim Sight-seer in Andover

Bradstreet, son of a non-conformist Lincolnshire minister and sometime steward to the Earl of Lincoln and Countess of Warwick, and Anne, his young wife of eighteen, daughter of Gov. Thomas Dudley, were passengers on the *Arbella*, landing at Salem with Governor Winthrop in 1630. They were a notable couple in the early history of the town and colony. He built a mill, where now are famous manufactories all around, he

HOME OF ANNE BRADSTREET, NORTH ANDOVER.

was "selectman" — a great office that, in the New England town, then and now ! — he was over sixty years in the colony's service, Secretary, Assistant, Deputy Governor, Governor, and Ambassador to the court of Charles II., after the Restoration. She was the first poet of the new world, her first publication, London, 1650, having the title — perhaps a bit of poetical license — "The Tenth Muse Sprung up in America, by a Gentlewoman in those Parts." From the eight children she

The Pilgrim Sight-seer in Andover

reared in the wilderness descended a numerous and remarkable progeny, illustrated by such names as Oliver Wendell Holmes, Richard H. Dana, Joseph S. Buckminster, and William Ellery Channing. Their homestead, burned in the year of the great fire in London, rebuilt in 1667, is still standing in North Andover (now a separate town), and well worth a visit.

A large British element has been constantly maintained by the immigration of families connected with the manufactures of the town. Three sturdy young Scotchmen, John and Peter Smith and John Dove, nearly eighty years ago sought their fortunes in the new world. They found them in Andover, and their long lives were a great part of the industrial, moral, and religious history of the town. With John Smith at the head, they built not only two villages around their flax mills; they built — in anti-slavery times — the Free Church; they built Memorial Hall, a free library for the town; they built on Andover Hill a library for the Theological Seminary, calling it in memory of their native town, Brechin Hall; they built the Tenement Schools in memory of their adopted town on "Andover Hill" in Brechin; they were builders for temperance, for freedom, for many a good cause in the old world as well as the new.

By another English family of earlier date buildings were set on Andover Hill which have been seen all over the world. George Phillips, of Norfolk, crossed the sea with Governor Winthrop, Governor Dudley, and Governor Bradstreet in 1630, and became the first minister of Watertown. His great-grandson, Samuel Phillips, was the first pastor of the South Parish Church, Andover, sixty years, 1711-71. His son, Hon. Samuel Phillips, lived at the North Parish, in the gambrel-roofed Phillips mansion, still standing near the Bradstreet house, and in later years the property and summer home of his descendant, Phillips Brooks. This man's son, Samuel Phillips, magistrate, judge, senator, lieutenant governor, settled in the South Parish at the beginning of the Revolution, made powder for Washington's army, and in the midst of the war founded Phillips Academy, in order, he wrote, "to learn youth the great end and real business of living." This academy, started with great faith and great sagacity, has grown to be one of the first preparatory schools in the land, and has often been called the "Rugby of America." At its centennial in 1878 over 10,000 pupils had been enrolled, the total number now reaching nearly 15,000, including men of eminent learning, fame and usefulness in every sphere of life's work.

Out of the academy, by the very terms of its far-seeing Constitution, grew, in 1808, Andover Theological Seminary, the first school of its kind in the world, the combined institutions owning the whole summit of Andover Hill — two hundred acres — for their present use and future growth. Over 3,000 men have been trained here, but no figures can measure the results of their labors, as during these ninety years they have gone into all the world, preaching Christ's gospel, founding other institutions, and raising up other teachers and preachers. Dr. Clark, founder of the Christian Endeavor, and C. M. Sheldon, author of "In His Steps," are of the more recent graduates.

Seventy years ago an Andover woman, of the same Phillips blood and benevolence, founded Abbot Academy, from which have gone out more than 4,000 educated women to bless the world.

Andover has been the mother of great societies and reforms. The first three seminary classes included Judson, Newell, Hall, Mills, and Richards. Their burning desire to go to the heathen and the conference of good men in a professor's house led to the formation of the American Board of Foreign Missions. The American Tract Society and the American Education Society were born here, and Andover men of that early day had an influential part in starting the national temperance and home missionary societies, the "Monthly Concert of Prayer for the conversion of the world," and the religious newspaper. The first editor of the *Boston Recorder* was an Andover schoolboy, and Professors Park and Edwards were consulting editors of *The Congregationalist* at its beginning in 1849.

For seventy years Andover was a notable center of theological publications, American and English. For a time it was the best if not the only place in the country for printing books requiring various fonts of Oriental type, and the famous "Codman Press," donated by Dr. John Codman (who studied at Edinburgh, preached in London and was the friend of Chalmers, Newton, and Burder), increased the advantage. Moses Stuart's Hebrew Grammar was printed in 1813, and Robinson's New Testament Lexicon in 1825. Stuart's Letters to Dr. Channing and his commentaries were well known in Great Britain. Woods, Porter, Park, Shedd, B. B. Edwards, Hackett, Phelps, Thayer, printed here works of solid value. Mr. Draper, still living at fourscore, published the *Bibliotheca Sacra* forty years, and over 150 other volumes, including the works of Whately, Henderson, Ellicott, Murphy, Lightfoot, and Perowne. It is estimated that over 400 books have been published in Andover, besides those written here by Mrs. Stowe, Miss Phelps, and others, but printed elsewhere.

If all these facts show that a small country town, quite aside from the great centers of commercial activity, has been privileged for a full century to bear a large and blessed part in molding the minds and lives of men throughout the world, and that by intellectual and moral forces alone — forces which are a heritage from our Puritan ancestors — our visitors may desire to identify a few sites of historic interest.

Two sites are prehistoric, and will interest geologists —

Indian Ridge, a "kame" first made famous by President Hitchcock (now reserved for a public park), and Pomp's Pond, the most noted "kettle-hole," perhaps, in the world. Here are also many "glacial scratches," and Prospect Hill is one of the best specimens of "drumlins" on the globe.

The School Street route from the station to the hill passes the Old South Church and Abbot Academy. By Main Street Memorial Hall is passed and, near the top of the hill, on the right, the house in the lower parlor of which, in 1832, Samuel F. Smith, a theological student, wrote "America," now a national hymn, sung wherever the national flag floats, to the same tune as "God Save the Queen!" Phillips Academy is on the right, then the long row of professors' residences. The second house, a modest one of brick, has been for sixty-three years the home of Professor Edwards A. Park, the eminent exponent of the "New England Theology," who has recently passed his ninetieth birthday. Farther on is Professor Moore's stately house, built for Dr. Griffin, and afterwards the residence of Dr. Porter, Dr. Justin Edwards, and Prof. Austin Phelps, whose essay, "My Study," records remarkable reminiscences of the southern wing. The small building adjoining it was the study of his daughter, Elizabeth Stuart Phelps. Dr. Woods lived next; then come the site of Judge Phillips' "mansion house" (unfortunately burned a few years ago), with its associations of Washington and Lafayette, the "old printing-house" (brick), and the home of Moses Stuart. Opposite that, now occupied by Professor Smyth, is the house where Oliver Wendell Holmes lived as a schoolboy, while just beyond, through the trees, is the old academy where he spoke his graduating piece in 1825. In nearly every house on this hill great men have lived, or boys have lodged who afterwards became great.

Retracing now our steps, we walk along the archway of elms, Brechin Hall at one end, the chapel at the other, passing the

The Pilgrim Sight-seer in Andover

three plain old seminary halls. Opposite the chapel is the stone house where Harriet Beecher Stowe lived, and wrote her later works. Behind the seminary is the aged oak of which Mrs. Stowe wrote, and into which Dr. Pearson climbed at the beginning of the century to survey the site of the future seminary. Close to it stood the old commons-house of the

HARRIET BEECHER STOWE'S HOME.

students, in which lived for a time Henry Obookiah, whose short, romantic life led to the changed history of the Hawaiian Islands. A few rods eastward is the God's acre where sleep in sacred quiet many of God's saints — Woods, Stuart, Phelps, Edwards, Dr. Taylor, Professor and Harriet Beecher Stowe, the cross of Scotch granite over the grave of Mrs. Stowe being copied from a cross, of ancient Iona design, which she had greatly admired on the estate of the Duke of Argyll. To the northward, across the field, are the Missionary Woods, once stretching to the pond, where walked and talked and prayed the first American missionaries.

Concord and Lexington

The visitor to Concord and Lexington stands on "holy ground" — ground made sacred forever by the lives lived and the lives sacrificed upon it. Here with all the certainty of foreordination Calvinism in theology bred democracy in politics. Here the strenuous, simple, God-fearing life of the pioneers of English stock developed men and women who dauntlessly faced the perils of revolt against the mother country, and gladly shed the first blood in that strife. Here through all the years from the original settlement in the seventeenth century down to the present time there have been men of culture, men of letters, who have derived from its quiet landscapes and rural delights that serenity of soul which has enabled them to do deeds and produce literature which will abide in memory so long as English is understood of men.

To the student of institutions, such as the town meeting, the public school, the free church, and the town library, Concord is an admirable laboratory of investigation. To the student of American literature it transcends all other towns of like size in its identification with the careers of such men as Emerson, Hawthorne, Thoreau, A. Bronson Alcott, and Ellery Channing, not to mention those like George William Curtis, Margaret Fuller, W. T. Harris and others, who have lived in the town for short periods of time.

To the patriot, the service rendered by the minutemen of the two towns in all of the wars in which the nation has been engaged, but more especially in the War of the Revolution, makes them shrines which he must visit, if he would do homage to valor and self-sacrifice.

The pilgrim journeying to these towns from Boston has his choice of two routes by rail (by the Boston & Maine, or by

The Pilgrim Sight-seer in Concord and Lexington

the Fitchburg, Railroad). If he decides on the former he will do well to take the electric cars either at Boston or Cambridge, which run over the old turnpike along which the British soldiers marched from Boston so confidently on the morning of that fateful day in April, 1775. All along the route on what is now known as Massachusetts Avenue he will see tablets marking the sites of minor engagements between the British troops and the American minutemen when the former were retreating to Boston. Leaving the electrics at Arlington Heights and taking the train, a few minutes' ride brings the traveler to the heart of Lexington village. *En route*, as he passes through the meadows of East Lexington, to the left of the track, may be seen the old Monroe Tavern, now a substantial residence of the old type, but prior to the Revolution a favorite resort of the British officers in Boston, and used after the battle of the 19th as a hospital. Proceeding to the village common, he will find it marked by two monuments celebrating the conflict; one a boulder, partly covered with vines, which denotes the spot where the head of the line of American minutemen stood when Captain Parker — grandfather of Theodore Parker, the eminent Boston radical preacher of a later generation — said to his men, "Stand your ground. Don't fire unless fired upon. But if they want to have a war, let it begin here!" The other monument, also partly covered with vines, bears a selection written by Rev. Jonas Clarke, the patriotic clergyman in whose parsonage home John Hancock and Samuel Adams were sleeping when aroused by Paul Revere on the morning of April 19. This inscription is written in the spread-eagle style of eloquence, more common at the time when it was composed than now. Making due allowance for this, it still remains an impressive eulogy.

About the common there still stand a few of the houses

which were there at the time of the fight. The home of Jonathan Harrington, to which he crawled, wounded and dying, is there. The old Buckman Tavern, which is in a fine state of preservation, faces the common. On the road leading to Bedford may be found the old parsonage, referred to above, in which Samuel Adams and John Hancock slept, and where Parson John Hancock and Parson Jonas Clarke each

THE PARSONAGE, LEXINGTON.

lived for more than fifty years. It is now the property of the Lexington Historical Society and is filled with memorials of the early life of the town, — portraits, furniture, wearing apparel and the like. This house, apart from its connection with characters so prominently identified with the political history of the time, is especially interesting because of its typical character as the home of two old-fashioned clergymen. Here Parson Hancock reared five children, and Parson Clarke

CHURCH AND PARSONAGE, BEDFORD.

twelve children, six of them daughters, four of whom became clergymen's wives.

The Town Hall of Lexington is interesting because it shelters the town Library and a collection of memorials of its citizens' share in the War of the Revolution and in the Civil War. Here may be seen the pistols of Major Pitcairn, commander of the English forces, which were captured with his horse on the retreat, and were afterward carried, through the Revolutionary War, by Gen. Israel Putnam. Here may be seen, too, several of the old flintlock muskets which the Lexington and Bedford farmers used so accurately and mercilessly. In the Town Hall, — the local parliament house, — where every male of requisite age is privileged to say his say and cast his vote on all questions of local administration, there is a spirited painting of the Battle of Lexington, by Henry Sandham.

Proceeding on the way to Concord by train, one arrives at a station situated in the low lands lying along the Concord River, the stream up and down which Thoreau plied his oars, and along which many a present-day canoeist threads his way, exploring the quiet reaches of a sinuous waterway, which now widens and now narrows and always satisfies one who likes a simple and unpretentious landscape, full of quiet beauty. Wending one's way toward the center of the village, one passes a tablet marking the site of the home of Rev. Peter Bulkeley, a Puritan minister from Bedfordshire, England, to whom, with Simon Willard, a merchant from Hawkshurst, in Kent, the tract was granted by Governor Winthrop in September, 1635. Bulkeley's father was a graduate of Cambridge University, England, and was a man of wealth and scholarship. At the age of fifty-two, together with a company of substantial English folk, the son set out for America, and became the real father and founder of the settlement at Concord, impressing his personal beliefs and habits upon the community in a very unusual way. His offspring were numerous, and his blood flows in the veins of many American families, the most notable of them being the Emersons of Concord, of whom, of course, Ralph Waldo Emerson was the most distinguished.

Turning to the left, as soon as the center of the town is gained, and proceeding northward, past pleasant homes hidden by trees and covered with vines, erelong one comes to The

THE OLD MANSE.

Old Manse, which stands back from the main highway at the end of an avenue of noble trees, chiefly ash, the gardens in the rear stretching down to the Concord River, and the whole setting of the place being one of unusual beauty. It was built in 1765, and at the time of the fight of 1775 was the home of the young pastor of the village church, William Emerson. From one of its western windows his wife looked out upon the fight between the American and the British troops at the bridge.

The Pilgrim Sight-seer in Concord and Lexington

This patriot preacher entered the service of the American army as chaplain, and died soon after enlistment. His widow became the wife of his successor, Rev. Ezra Ripley, and they lived in this building for sixty years. It was in this house that Ralph Waldo Emerson, then a guest of the Ripley family, wrote his book "Nature," occupying as his study the room on the second floor, from which his grandmother saw the fight. Nathaniel Hawthorne resided here during the first four years after his marriage with Sophia Peabody, in 1842, and his book "Mosses from an Old Manse" has made classic much of the atmosphere and tradition which then lingered about the old house. When it was built it was the largest and most pretentious house in the village and for a long time was the only one with three stories. It stands to-day one of the choicest specimens of the early Colonial architecture, and, like the Hancock-Clarke house, in Lexington, is interesting because of its identification with the early ecclesiastical life of the Colony. Within its walls have been sheltered for brief and for long periods many who in the early days gave shape to the spiritual and political ideals, first of the Colony and then of the nation.

Just beyond this historic and picturesque structure is the site of the battle between the Americans and British. One approaches it through an avenue of trees, down through the vista of which one sees D. C. French's statue of The Minute Man. The topography of the land now is not exactly as it was at the time of the contest, but is essentially the same. As one looks off over the meadows of green beside the slowly moving stream, upon the gentle hill-slopes to the homes of the well-to-do farmers and merchants, he is charmed with the beauty of the landscape and the quiet of it all, and it is difficult to associate the spot with the beginnings of a war that involved so much bloodshed and heartbreak. One has to turn to the descriptions of the battle which are to be found in all the guidebooks,

BATTLE BRIDGE CONCORD.

THE MINUTE MAN, CONCORD BATTLEFIELD.

The Pilgrim Sight-seer in Concord and Lexington

to realize that he is, indeed, standing where

> The embattled farmers stood
> And fired the shot heard round the world.

Or the monument which marks the spot and bears the following inscription will make it equally vivid: —

> HERE
> On the 19th of April, 1775,
> Was Made the First Forcible Resistance of
> British Aggression.
> On the opposite bank stood the American militia,
> Here stood the invading army.
> And on this spot the first of the enemy fell
> in the War of the Revolution,
> which gave Independence to these United States.
> In gratitude to God, and in the love of Freedom,
> This monument was erected,
> A. D. 1836.

Mr. French's statue was the first important undertaking of one who has since become one of the recognized masters of the art of sculpture in this country. It was done when he was but twenty-five years of age, and, taking everything into consideration, is a most satisfactory representation of the typical American farmer of the period, who, like Cincinnatus, was ready to leave at an instant call the life of peace and industry for one of strife in defense of what he believed to be the just demands of patriotism.

Returning to the center of the town, the present Town Hall, the old Wright Tavern, built in 1747, the meeting house of the Unitarian Church, in a former edifice of which the first Provincial Congress of delegates from the towns of Massachusetts met in October, 1774, and the ancient burying ground are to be found. Continuing on the highway to the east one sees house after house, built under the shelter of the low hill, which were formerly occupied by men who participated in the stirring scenes of the Revolution. One of them is now the headquarters of the Concord Antiquarian Society, and contains, among other exceedingly interesting and instructive relics, a pallet and desk which Thoreau used.

A short distance beyond this, on the highway to Lexington, by the side of the turnpike over which the British retreated, stands the plain but neat and attractive wooden house, painted white, with green blinds, and sheltered partially by noble pines and elms, the home of Ralph Waldo Emerson, and now in the possession of and occupied by his descendants. Formerly this was the mecca of more Englishmen visiting the United States than any other haunt in the country. And what is true of the past is probably still true not only of this house but of the town of Concord, as compared with other towns of New England. But with the death of Emerson the personality that made the home interesting and vital departed and the visitor of to-day must be contented with gazing at its exterior and with a visit of homage to Emerson's grave, in Sleepy Hollow Cemetery, of which a word later.

Continuing the journey eastward, the next home of importance is that once occupied by A. Bronson Alcott — the mystic — and his daughter, Louisa M. Alcott, one of the most popular American writers of stories for young people, whose life of early privation and whose brave struggle to provide the necessities and luxuries of life for her parents is one of the most pathetic narratives in the history of American women of letters. To those interested in the transcendental movement in New England, and who are conversant with the part played in the movement by Mr. Alcott, this house will have interest, but the majority of those visiting it know of it and care for it because of Miss Alcott's life there. Near the Alcott house

MERRIAM'S CORNER, CONCORD.

is the little unpainted, wooden building where for ten years the Concord School of Philosophy held its sessions.

Just beyond this is the house called The Wayside, in which Hawthorne lived during his second period of sojourn in Concord, from 1852 to the end of his life, with intervals spent abroad. Here he wrote "Tanglewood Tales," "Dr. Grimshawe's Secret," and most of his later works. To the few he liked he was accessible, but his life here, on the whole, was one of reserve and seclusion. The house is now owned and occupied by Mrs. Daniel C. Lothrop, who as a writer of stories for youth, under the *nom de plume* of Margaret Sydney, has won considerable reputation.

A short distance beyond the end of the ridge which runs back of these houses is Merriam's Corner, where the first attack upon the retreating British column was made by the American minutemen — an attack which was continued all along the way back to Boston, through Lexington, Menotomy (now Arlington), North Cambridge, Somerville, to Charlestown Neck, where the British came under the protection of the guns of the British ships of war. Their loss during the day was 73 killed, 174 wounded, and 26 missing.

Returning to the center of the village, and taking a road leading to the north, it is but a short walk to the beautiful Sleepy Hollow Cemetery, wherein are buried Emerson, Hawthorne and some of his children, A. Bronson Alcott and his daughter Louisa, Henry D. Thoreau, Samuel E. Rockwood, and Sherman Hoar, and many other lesser known but gifted and patriotic former residents of the town. Emerson's grave, 'neath lofty pines, is marked by a superb boulder of pink quartz, bearing the following lines from his poem, "The Problem": —

> The passive Master lent his hand
> To the vast soul that o'er him planned.

The Pilgrim Sight-seer in Concord and Lexington

It is difficult to exaggerate the solemn beauty of this pine-crowned ridge, in whose soil rest the remains of these famous dead. Rarely is a more appropriate natural setting for such memorials to be had, and seldom do the living show such restraint in refraining from marring the natural beauty of a lovely spot.

Of all the natives of Concord — Emerson and Hawthorne were not natives — none is more famous now than the long-misunderstood Thoreau, whose quaint birthplace is pictured

THOREAU'S BIRTHPLACE.

above. In the center of the village he lived for a time, and the house he then occupied now bears his name. But he is more intimately connected, in the minds of his readers, with Walden Pond and its sylvan beauties and seclusion. Thither all devout admirers of his philosophy of life, his insight into nature, will journey. It is about twenty minutes' ride out of town, off to the southeast.

How rich the town has been in men of letters and men of

action one scarcely realizes until he has carefully inspected the alcoves of the town Library, where are displayed in serried order the books written by Concord authors, and the portraits, busts, and other memorabilia of the authors, divines, soldiers, and statesmen who have given fame to the town. Here in this Valhalla one sees an agent at work vitally influencing the thought and aspiration of the present generation of townsfolk, and one that will become increasingly influential as its riches increase. Youths cannot go in and out of its doors, week in and week out, in search of books, without at the same time deriving some inspiration from the settings among which the books are placed. Nor can transient visitors leave the place quite the same persons as when they entered, for it is as if one were suddenly carried up to a rarer atmosphere, or suddenly subjected to the focused light of countless stars. "Plain living and high thinking" has been the rule in Concord from earliest times, and is the most priceless inheritance of its present folk. Near enough to Boston to keep in touch with its larger life and thus escape provinciality, the town has been far enough away to live its own life and keep its own lofty standards of democracy and literacy.

THE CONGREGATIONAL HOUSE

For a quarter of a century the headquarters of Congregationalism in Boston were at the corner of Beacon and Somerset Streets. In 1871 the American Congregational Association purchased the Somerset Club House and an adjoining estate, reconstructing them so that they were suitable for occupancy by the various Congregational organizations, which, up to that time, had been domiciled in several buildings in different streets. The first Congregational House was dedicated February 12, 1873.

For many years this building seemed spacious and was regarded as ample for its purposes. But Congregationalism grew with the city and the country, and when the first International Council in 1891 voted that the second council should be held in the United States — of course looking to Boston as the place — the question of having a new Congregational House was already being seriously considered. The approach of the meeting increased the interest in providing a new building and probably hastened its erection.

The land on which the Congregational House now stands, with the other lots as far as Park Street, was the property of the town of Boston, and was sold by it to Thomas Amory about one hundred years ago. A double house was built on this lot by a Mr. Payne, a representative of one of Boston's oldest

The Congregational House

families, and that house came into the possession of the Whitmore family about twenty-five years ago; thence in 1896 it became the property of the American Congregational Association. It is now No. 14 Beacon Street.

The architects of the new building were Messrs. Rutan, Shepley, and Coolidge, and the corner-stone was laid with appropriate ceremonies November 27, 1897. The late Dr. C. A. Berry, of Wolverhampton, England, made one of the addresses on that occasion. The edifice was so far completed by August 1, 1898, that some of the rooms were occupied, and before the end of that month nearly all the occupants of the old building had moved into the new one. (*See Frontispiece.*)

The relief sculptures on the *façade* of the second story have an interesting history. They were begun, under the direction of the building committee and of Rev. E. G. Porter, who conceived and suggested the designs, by a young Spaniard; but on the outbreak of war between his country and ours, he abandoned his work, and it was completed by a Swiss. The four subjects represented by historical scenes in the founding of New England are Law, Religion, Education, and Philanthropy. The tablets are seen to the best advantage in the afternoon light from the opposite side of the street at or near Bowdoin Street. Photographs of them have been reproduced, in convenient form, with descriptions, by *The Congregationalist*.

There are two stories below the entrance on Beacon Street, and in the lowest story is the well-lighted and attractive Pilgrim Hall, seating about three hundred persons. The remaining rooms on this and the next floor above are for storage and packing and general purposes. The entrance floor, on the right, is occupied by the bookstore of the Congregational Sunday-School and Publishing Society. The library, with its spacious reading room, has the place of honor on the second floor; and connected with it is the room containing a very

LAW

"Two of the scenes were taken from the Old Colony and two from that of the Bay.

"The first controlling sentiment which was exhibited by our forefathers even before they landed, was the necessity of a recognized government to guard their fondly-cherished liberties. They made admirable provision for this in the solemn compact which was drawn up on board the Mayflower in Cape Cod harbor and promptly signed by the forty-one men of the little company. Here the scene was a perfect embodiment of the idea to be portrayed, viz.: the majesty of law.

Religion

"*Next came the most characteristic trait of the fathers — the expression of their religious faith. Several scenes might have been chosen for this. The one preferred was the remarkable observance of the Sabbath by the exploring party on Clark's Island the day before they set foot on Plymouth Rock.*

EDUCATION

"The third subject — education — offered itself at once as the ever-present handmaid of religion in New England, and the appropriation of the General Court, Oct. 28, 1636, for 'a school or college,' was an event of such extraordinary interest in itself and in its consequences that it was selected without hesitation. Boston has this honor, as the courts which had met at Cambridge (Newe Towne) during a part of the previous year sat in Boston from May, 1636, till May, 1637, when they returned to Cambridge for a short time and were there when the committee of six magistrates and six ministers was appointed (Nov. 20, 1637) 'to take order for a college at Newtown.' The name of Harvard was adopted the following year.

PHILANTHROPY

"*The fourth tablet is intended to set forth the beneficent fruits of the Congregational faith and practice; not in an exclusive, but in an historical, sense, for which, indeed, the building itself exists, with the various denominational societies sheltered within its walls. The evangelic spirit, drawn directly from the New Testament and encouraged by an enlightened mind and a consecrated heart, finds expression in missions of all kinds at home and abroad. The efforts of the apostle Eliot to establish 'praying villages' among his beloved Indians furnishes the theme for this, and he is represented as preaching to them at Waban's wigwam on the hill at Nonantum in 1642. No better example of true philanthropy could be found in the annals of any country, ancient or modern.*" — EDWARD G. PORTER, *in* The Congregationalist.

THE READING ROOM, CONGREGATIONAL HOUSE.

The Congregational House

interesting collection of Bibles, manuscripts, and other treasures gathered by Mr. S. B. Pratt. The third, fourth, and fifth floors are mostly occupied as offices by various parties who rent these rooms from the Association. On the sixth and seventh floors are the rooms of the benevolent societies and organizations administering the work of the denomination. The eighth floor is occupied by *The Congregationalist*, by Deacon Thomas Todd and his company of compositors, and by the editorial forces of the Sunday-School and Publishing Society. The list of organizations and persons domiciled within the building, connected with Congregational interests, is as follows : —

American Board of Commissioners for Foreign Missions........Room 708
Woman's Board of Missions................................702–707
American Missionary Association..................................615
Boston Seaman's Friend Society...................................601
Woman's Seaman's Friend Society..................................601
Boston City Missionary Society...................................602
Woman's Home Missionary Society..................................607
Massachusetts Home Missionary Society............................609
Congregational Board of Pastoral Supply..........................610
Congregational Church Building Society...........................611
National Council Headquarters, Dr. H. A. Hazen, Secretary........611
Congregational Education Society.................................612
Congregational Sunday-School and Publishing Society..............805
The Congregationalist..803

Library and Building

AMERICAN CONGREGATIONAL ASSOCIATION

This is the Society that owns and cares for the Congregational House, the headquarters of our six national benevolent societies. Three of the six, it is true, have their main offices in New York, but Boston is the chief source of supply in each case. The Association holds the position of a keystone in an arch ; destroy the Congregational House, and the societies would have as little mutual connection as they had before 1873, when the old House was occupied. But the prosperity of the Association carries with it a direct benefit to all the benevolent organizations. For when the House is fully occupied, the net income will be available to reduce the rentals charged to these societies ; and in time, their rooms will be free of all charge. That day is hastened by every gift to the treasury of the Association.

One important department of this Association is the Congregational Library, which occupies the second and third floors in the rear of the House. Established in 1853, to preserve " the religious history and literature of New England," and ever keeping that object foremost, it has enlarged its scope with its increasing growth. At present there are upwards of 40,000 volumes and nearly 50,000 pamphlets. The field covered embraces biblical, theological, and general literature, history, biography, genealogy, sociology, and education, with a large representation of periodicals, religious and secular. These books are kept in a fireproof stack of the most approved pattern. A beautiful reading room contains the leading reviews and magazines, with more than a thousand reference books. Another room is devoted to relics, and a third to the fine collection of Bibles and objects illustrating the Bible, presented by Mr. S. Brainard Pratt. The rooms are always open to visitors ; the books are designed for reference rather than circulation. Contributions for new books are always welcome.

Foreign Missions

THE AMERICAN BOARD OF COMMISSIONERS FOR FOREIGN MISSIONS

ORGANIZED 1810   INCORPORATED 1812

The object is to propagate the gospel among the unevangelized nations and communities, by means of preachers, teachers, Bible readers, other helpers, and the press, and to establish self-supporting, self-governing, self-propagating, Christian institutions of every kind.

It is the agent of the Congregational churches of America in the work of Foreign Missions. After ninety years of honorable history it reports twenty missions: one each in Micronesia, Hawaiian Islands, Japan; three in Papal lands, Austria, Spain, and Mexico; four in China,— North, South, Shansi, and Foochow; three in India, — Marathi, Madura, — and Ceylon; three in Africa, — Zulu, East, and West Central; and four in Turkey, — Eastern, Western, Central, and European.

In these missions the Board has stationed 539 missionaries, men and women; these missionaries are reinforced by about 3,000 trained native helpers; these toilers have already equipped 465 Christian churches, and 47,000 members are enrolled. The net gain last year was above ten per cent.

The problems of Christian education are also at the front. The schools of every grade number 1,270, with an enrollment of over 56,000 pupils. These include eighteen theological seminaries and thirteen collegiate institutions.

The Board also supports the medical missionary, the printing press, the Sunday-school, and the Christian Endeavor.

The Woman's Board, Boston; the Woman's Board of the Interior, Chicago; and the Woman's Board of the Pacific, San Francisco, are auxiliary.

The regular publications are the *Missionary Herald*, monthly, and *Mission Dayspring* for children. *Life and Light* and *Mission Studies* are published monthly by the Woman's Boards.

Foreign Missions

THE WOMAN'S BOARD OF MISSIONS

The Woman's Board of Missions, acting in connection with the American Board of Commissioners for Foreign Missions, was organized in Boston in January, 1868, through the instrumentality of a small company of women in the city and vicinity. Its purpose was the Christianization of women in foreign lands carried on under the recommendation or approval of the officers of the American Board. During the first year it assumed the support of seven lady missionaries, eleven native Bible-women. At the present time it has under its care 129 missionaries, 33 boarding-schools, 290 day schools in whole or in part, and 164 native Bible-women. The constituency of the Board is composed of the women in the Congregational churches east of Ohio in the United States, there being two other similar Woman's Boards, the Woman's Board of the Interior, with headquarters in Chicago, and of the Pacific, with headquarters in San Francisco.

Since the American Board had an entrance into the churches in the usual way it was thought best for the Woman's Board to form local auxiliary societies among the women and children in the churches, which were afterwards grouped around convenient centers in organizations called branches. It now has twenty-four branches, comprising more than seventeen hundred auxiliaries. In these various societies upwards of twelve thousand meetings are held each year for prayer and missionary information. To supply this information the Board issues a monthly magazine, *Life and Light*, a children's periodical jointly with the American Board, *The Mission Dayspring*, besides thousands of leaflets and manuscripts, letters and papers.

The receipts of the Board for the first year were $5,033.42. The present annual income is between $130,000 and $140,000. The total receipts for the thirty years is nearly $3,000,000.

Home Missions

THE HOME MISSIONARY SOCIETIES

THE MASSACHUSETTS HOME MISSIONARY SOCIETY

The Massachusetts Home Missionary Society, organized May 28, 1799, became auxiliary to the Congregational Home Missionary Society in 1832. In the hundred years it has spent in Massachusetts $1,500,000, and sent $2,500,000 to New York for work in the West, and $2,000,000 has been sent directly from Massachusetts to the national society. In all $6,000,000, of which $4,500,000 went to the West.

Our churches through the State Society are (1) aiding old churches in country towns mostly to maintain the preaching of the gospel, (2) helping new enterprises in cities and large towns, and (3) providing that to those recently come among us the gospel shall be preached in their own language.

In carrying out this work the Society has aided 367 churches and missions in the State, and has 144 now on its list. Last year grants were made for work among Armenians, Finns, French, Germans, Greeks, Italians, Norwegians, Poles, and Swedes. Rev. JOSHUA COIT, Sec.; Rev. EDWIN B. PALMER, Treas.

THE CONGREGATIONAL HOME MISSIONARY SOCIETY

The Congregational Home Missionary Society, including its twelve auxiliaries, in its last fiscal year aided in the maintenance of more than eighteen hundred missionaries, by whom the gospel was regularly preached at nearly three thousand churches and stations. Of these missionaries 212 preached in foreign languages.

Of the 5,620 Congregational churches in the United States more than four fifths are the fruits of home missions, above three thousand having been brought to self-support. In the seventy-three years of the Society's work its receipts have reached a total of $18,482,044. J. B. CLARK, D.D., W. CHOATE, D.D., Sec's; Mr. W. B. HOWLAND, Treas.

Home Missions

WOMAN'S HOME MISSIONARY ASSOCIATION

Woman's work for home missions is an heirloom in our household of faith, present methods being simply an adaptation to present needs.

We have no roll call of those colonial dames accustomed to set aside measures of meal toward the support of a young missionary college on the Charles; but their gift was accepted, with that of Anne Radcliffe, in the name of "Christ and the church."

In early days, sewing bees led a desultory life, in accordance with local or patriotic emergencies. Beginning this century with the New Hampshire Cent Society, founded (1804) by Madam McFarland of blessed memory, women's efforts have kept steady pace with the great missionary movements. Some circles, whose distinctive work has been the preparing of barrels for the frontier, have passed their seventy-fifth anniversaries.

In 1880 the Woman's Home Missionary Association was formed for the purpose of enlisting all the women of the Congregational churches in prayer and effort for Home Missions. Doing its work on the field with or through the five national societies, it gives each contributor the interest of a stockholder in all the Home Missionary enterprises of the denomination.

Pledges for salaries and scholarships, for churches, parsonages, colleges, and Sunday-schools, besides the constant supply of constant missionary needs, all serve to keep the workers at home in close touch with the workers at the front.

The Auxiliaries and clusters of Auxiliaries, known as Alliances or Neighborhood Meetings, have as great variety in form and methods as in gifts. The tendency of such fellowship is a "leveling up" in the standard of work all along the line.

The office of the Association is at 607 Congregational House, where visitors to the Council will be made welcome.

Church and Parsonage Building

CONGREGATIONAL CHURCH BUILDING SOCIETY

Headquarters, 105 East 22d Street, New York, N. Y. Been at the work of church and parsonage building forty-six years, plus. Expects to be at it till the kingdom comes. Has helped buy or build more than 3,000 houses of worship, and some sixty-one homes for ministers.

Its methods are live methods; its money is live money. It goes out to help one church; comes back and goes out again to help another church. More than $700,000 of its output has been used more than once. The per cent of financial loss is small, and is more than made up by non-forfeitable investments in Christian character formed and trained for service.

This one of our six arms of field service is emphatically our centralizing, focalizing agency. It localizes the thought and actual dwelling of God in our smaller and larger communities.

It gives opportunity for the largest and least gifts to genuine benevolence. What grander benevolence than helping to localize God in a community? More than $2,600,000 has been disbursed among 3,000 churches.

The work of this Society is thoroughly missionary. It keeps four men as busy as other duties will allow, preaching the gospel of the growing Kingdom, the same as they and others preach the gospel of repentance and faith in the Lord Jesus Christ. Rev. George A. Hood, of Boston, has the six New England States to keep alive to this vital work. Rev. C. H. Taintor, of Chicago, and Mrs. Taintor, look after thirteen of our great interior states. Rev. H. H. Wikoff has three Pacific coast states, beside Arizona, Idaho, Montana, and Utah; 260 other men have an eye to the development and permanent growth of the work on this matchless field for Christian enterprise. The assets of the aided churches are more than $14,000,000. The tide is rising.

For Oppressed Races

THE AMERICAN MISSIONARY ASSOCIATION

The American Missionary Association represents the work of church extension and Christian education throughout the South and West. Its missions are planted among the Negroes and Highlanders in the South, the Indians, Chinese, and Japanese in the West, and the Alaskans in the remote northwestern territory. The Association hopes to enter Porto Rico with a band of Christian teachers and evangelists this autumn.

The methods of mission work pursued by the Association include the Christian school and college and the organized Christian church. Industrial training, of which the American Missionary Association was the pioneer in the South, has been maintained and developed since 1867. In many of the schools complete courses of instruction in manual training prepare the students for their life work. In the normal schools of the Association especial attention is given to training teachers to furnish the educational leaders of their people.

Six chartered institutions under the direction of competent faculties present full college curriculums. The public schools of the South are largely supplied among the colored people by those trained in these institutions. The Highlands occupy the very heart of the country, covering an area five hundred miles long by two hundred and fifty broad.

Among the Indians the Association maintains three central schools and thirty out-stations. At Cape Prince of Wales, Alaska, a mission is maintained among the Eskimo. A herd of reindeer affords a unique but important feature of this mission station.

Among the Chinese and Japanese in America twenty schools are conducted.

District Offices: Boston, Mass., 615 Congregational House, Rev. George H. Gutterson, Secretary. Chicago, Ill., 153 La Salle St., Rev. J. E. Roy, D.D., Secretary.

Education

CONGREGATIONAL EDUCATION SOCIETY

This society is the confluence of three streams of distinguished Congregational history. On December 7, 1816, was organized "The American Society for Educating Pious Youth for the Gospel Ministry." On June 29, 1843, began "The Society for the Promotion of Collegiate and Theological Education at the West." These were united, March 9, 1874, as "The American College and Education Society." On November 3, 1879, was organized "The New West Education Commission," whose schools have vigorously and heroically counteracted Mormon and Spanish-Catholic church influence; and which was united with the older society in 1893. The elemental titles of this comprehensive organization illustrate its work: Scholarships for theological students with an enrollment of 8,000 names; Christian colleges and academies brilliantly starring the West with more than fifty radiant lights; the early inculcation of the freedom and truth of the Christian faith. Those ideas most akin to the genius of Congregationalism are emphasized; the leadership of the Christian pulpit; national character built up by education guided by the highest ideals; and the defense of a Biblical faith, rationally interpreted, and imparted to the opening minds of children still in the twilight of civilization. The Society has shown wise adaptability to changed conditions: shifting emphasis from *number* to *quality*, in ministerial product; conquering a sure place amid legislated public school life; efficiently organizing state enterprise for advancing Christian educational interests; and so relating itself to the institutions under its care as to aid and guide, without infringing upon the liberty and authority of the governing board of each. Its President is William H. Willcox, D.D., of Malden, Mass., and its Vice-President, John Henry Barrows, D.D., President of Oberlin University.

Sunday-School Work

THE CONGREGATIONAL SUNDAY-SCHOOL AND PUBLISHING SOCIETY

This Society was organized in 1832, as the Massachusetts Sabbath-School Society. In 1854 the Congregational Board of Publication was merged into it and the double name was assumed. Both societies had published books and tracts. The society that publishes is, naturally, the society that distributes.

In 1883 it underwent a radical reorganization, receiving new elements of strength in both departments. The employment of Sunday-school missionaries was begun, those in charge of states being called Superintendents. Their number has increased to about forty. They labor to organize Sunday-schools in needy places, both in person and through the aid of pastors and others. They do evangelistic work where it is possible. They put the schools organized into relation with some near church. They do all they can within their various fields to increase the interest in and efficiency of the Sunday-school work in our churches. They organize annually about 500 schools, and aid 1,500. Over 700 Congregational churches have grown from the seed they have thus sown.

Meanwhile, since that same date, the Business Department has grown from a capital of $39,000 to one of $125,000, exclusive of its plates, engravings, etc., and sales of $100,000 annually have grown to over $260,000 a year. Its periodicals have reached a circulation of about two thirds of a million, and the profits of its business enable it to make large annual appropriations to the Missionary Department. It maintains large bookstores in Boston and Chicago, and aims to provide our churches and their people — and, indeed, all people — with all books published and sold by reputable houses, at prices at least as low as others, while in the line of church and Sunday-school requisites it aims to provide everything that is needed.

Work Among Seamen

BOSTON SEAMAN'S FRIEND SOCIETY

Among the oldest of our benevolent institutions is the Boston Seaman's Friend Society, Rev. Alexander McKenzie, D.D., President. It was an outgrowth of a society for the Moral and Religious Improvement of Seamen, founded in 1812, and was organized in Dr. Beecher's church in 1827. It has seen near three fourths of a century of honored and useful service. First it had a Chapel and Home at Fort Hill, later at the North End.

In 1893, by generous aid of our churches, the valuable property of the historic Cockerel Church, 287 Hanover Street, was purchased. Here is now the chief center of work done by this Society for the 160,000 seamen who annually visit this port and face the temptations and perils of a great city. Here is a daily resort for seamen, with books, papers, magazines, and writing material for their use. Here bands of good women meet seamen socially. Here are temperance meetings, with varied entertainments given by Endeavor Societies, and the famous sailors' suppers given by our largest churches. Here sailors in distress find shelter, food, clothing, care, and kind treatment, until they are able to reship. After one of the great storms last winter a hundred shipwrecked men, sent up from its important mission at Vineyard Haven, had this care. Here Chaplain Nickerson and his assistants meet seamen with a hearty welcome and good counsel every day in the week, winning many of them to a Christian life. The influence and blessing of the work extends to all seas and shores.

The efficiency of the Society has been greatly increased by the coöperation of the Woman's Seaman's Friend Society.

A debt of $10,000 still remains upon the property. As soon as this is provided for and an equal sum is secured for needed improvements, the Society will be in a position to do a much larger work.

Work Among Seamen

WOMAN'S SEAMAN'S FRIEND SOCIETY

In January, 1895, this Society was organized with thirty-two members, in response to an earnest appeal from the Boston Seaman's Friend Society for the coöperation of the women of the Congregational churches of Boston and vicinity in its work.

Mrs. Frederick O. White was elected President, and the Society was incorporated in October. Its membership has since then increased to nearly five hundred annual contributors and active workers. There are twenty-three life members, whose fees constitute a fund for reading-room supplies.

The work of the Society is various. The deft fingers of the women fashion mufflers, wristers, helmets, and comfort bags.

The influence and Christian sympathy of women are given in personal work for seamen at the morning prayer-meetings, and at the weekly social teas, where ladies meet the sailor with music, games, books, and magazines, and with light refreshments.

The Society takes a lively interest in the Naval Hospital at Chelsea, to which it has given an organ and hymn books. It has organized Sunday afternoon services, conducted mainly by Christian Endeavor Societies. It also sends fruits, flowers, and jellies to the sick, and gives some fine concerts to the convalescents. The Library Committee selects suitable books for the permanent library and the loan libraries; and the Correspondence Committee follows the sailor to distant lands with letters of good cheer and Christian sympathy, and receives from him in return replies which show the value of the work done, and that he feels there is a loving tie that binds him to those on shore who are truly interested in his welfare.

This work is world-wide, a missionary work in its widest scope, embracing both home and foreign endeavor, and should engage the prayers and lively interest of every Christian.

THE CONGREGATIONAL BOARD OF PASTORAL SUPPLY

This Board is maintained and controlled by the General Association of the Congregational Churches of Massachusetts. It is an agency which acts in an advisory way with respect to pastoral settlements wherever it is called upon to do it. It does nothing unless it is called upon. It has no shadow of authority over the churches, but it is itself responsible to the churches. This fact of complete public responsibility is characteristic and controlling. Our business is to set before churches clear and impartial and truthful testimonies relative to ministers concerning whom they make inquiry. While we do this always with a sense of obligation first to the churches, we aim to do it also with fairness and kindness toward the ministers respecting whom inquiries are made. We designate and engage men as candidates for the pastorate in behalf of any church that may so desire us.

Our work has been large almost from the first and is steadily increasing. We have information carefully collected relative to a very considerable proportion of all the Congregational ministers in the United States. During the year ending with the first of May, 1899, committees representing 152 churches conferred or corresponded with our office relative to pastoral settlements. The larger part of these churches were in Massachusetts; but our work extended to twenty-five other states and territories and reached to Nova Scotia and South Africa.

We also furnish occasional or temporary supplies for pulpits as they may be called for. A small fee is charged for service rendered to ministers living outside of Massachusetts.

Rev. DeWitt S. Clark, D.D., Chairman of Board of Directors; Herbert N. Ackerman, Treasurer; Rev. Charles B. Rice, Secretary, Room 610, Congregational House.

PART II

The International Council

Congregational Club
Retrospect and Prospect
Committees
Program of the Council
List of Delegates
Pilgrim Sight-seer's Calendar

ALBERT H. PLUMB, D.D.
President of the Congregational Club.

Congregational Club

In this organization have been gathered in pleasant fellowship not only nearly all the local pastors but a large proportion of the substantial business and professional men from about ninety churches in and around the city. Its present registration is about 450. Its purpose is to promote a more intimate acquaintance, and advance the general interest of Congregationalism. It was a pioneer in the field when organized in 1869, but since then not less than fifty-three other clubs in different sections of the country have been formed. During its thirty years' history the Club has listened, at its monthly meetings, to some of the most distinguished men in the country, while the list of subjects considered includes a large variety of important and timely themes. Twice a year the ladies are invited, and those occasions are always notable ones. The presidency usually alternates, from year to year, between a minister and a layman. This year, which marks the completion of thirty years of Club life, the president is Rev. A. H. Plumb, D.D., for twenty-seven years pastor of the Walnut Avenue Congregational Church, in Roxbury.

Soon after Boston was decided upon as the place of meeting for the International Council a committee of the Club considered what part it might have in the entertainment. It reported in favor of assuming, in coöperation with the local churches, the entire responsibility, and the Club voted heartily and unanimously to act as hosts. A committee of nine was appointed to perfect all necessary details. The Club itself will be in evidence on the second Wednesday evening during the session of the Council, when it has invited the delegates to a reception and banquet, which will probably be one of the most important social functions of the entire Council.

SAMUEL B. CAPEN, Esq.

Chairman of the General Committee of Arrangements and of the Executive Committee and of the Committee of the Congregational Club.

COMMITTEE OF THE CONGREGATIONAL CLUB
Appointed for Entertainment of the
INTERNATIONAL CONGREGATIONAL COUNCIL.

Chairman, Mr. SAMUEL B. CAPEN.

Vice-Chairman, Rev. WILLIAM E. BARTON, D.D.

Secretary, JOHN H. COLBY, Esq.

Treasurer, Mr. WILLIAM H. BLOOD.

Finance Committee.

Rev. D. W. WALDRON.

Mr. JACOB P. BATES.
Mr. FRANK W. STEARNS.
Mr. ALPHONSO S. COVEL.
Hon. ARTHUR H. WELLMAN.
Mr. SAMUEL USHER.
Mr. FRANK WOOD.

Transportation and Excursion.

Mr. WILLIAM F. WHITTEMORE.

Rev. WILLIAM E. BARTON, D.D.
Rev. EDWARD G. PORTER, D.D.
Hon. ARTHUR A. MAXWELL.
JOHN H. COLBY, Esq.
Mr. JOSEPH P. WARREN.

Entertainment Committee.

Rev. EDWARD S. TEAD.

Rev. GEORGE H. FLINT.
Rev. ELLIS MENDELL.
Rev. WILLIAM S. KELSEY.
Rev. ROBERT A. McFADDEN.
Rev. FRANK E. RAMSDELL.
Rev. CHARLES H. BEALE, D.D.

Printing Committee.

Rev. HOWARD A. BRIDGMAN.

Mr. FRANK P. SHUMWAY.
FRED L. NORTON, Esq.
Mr. ARTHUR W. KELLY.
Rev. G. R. W. SCOTT, D.D.

Music Committee.

Rev. MARSHALL M. CUTTER.
Prof. JUNIUS W. HILL.

SAMUEL JOHNSON, Esq.

One of the functions of the International Council anticipated with special interest is the collation and reception at the Vendome, Friday, September 22. It is an expression of the hospitality of the Congregational churches of Boston to the visiting delegates, to the religious organizations, and to representative citizens of the Commonwealth. It was conceived, planned, and provided for by MR. SAMUEL JOHNSON. Being warned that he might not live to see it, he carefully completed arrangements for it, with instructions that they should be carried out, in case he should die, as though he were living.

His plans for this occasion illustrate his character. He at first expressed the wish that his name should not be mentioned in connection with the reception. He desired that it should appear as the act of the churches. Always thoughtful for others, broad in his plans, and generous in carrying them out, he sought the larger good without self-consciousness. No layman could better stand as the representative of the Christian business men of Boston. Through his whole life he was identified with the Old South, the oldest and the leading Congregational church of the city. Always loyal to his pastor and his church, he wisely promoted the interests of the denomination and of the whole Christian church. With unblemished integrity, large and successful business experience, a kindness of spirit which beyond justice honored all claims on his service, a citizen valued and beloved, he passed to the life beyond suddenly and peacefully, Sunday morning, August 13, 1899, at the age of seventy-three years. He rests from his labors, and his works follow him.

Retrospect and Prospect

The Second International Congregational Council — the first on American soil — is the natural successor of the one held in London in July, 1891, composed of over three hundred delegates from all over the world. The three men who had thought and conferred most regarding the desirability of such a gathering were Drs. H. M. Dexter and A. H. Ross, of America, and Dr. Alexander Hannay, of England. Only Dr. Ross lived to see the idea realized. That body was in session eight days, and considered many subjects of large and timely concern. Its chairman was the late Dr. R. W. Dale, of Birmingham. Prominent members of the British delegation were Principals Fairbairn, Reynolds, and Simon, and Rev. Drs. Allon, Barrett, Brown, Hall, McKennal, Parker, and Rogers. Prominent Americans were Presidents Northrop, Slocum, and Angell, and Drs. Quint, Stearns, Boynton, Bradford, Goodwin, Hazen, and Taylor.

At the London Council it was the general opinion that Boston was the proper city for the next international gathering. Samuel B. Capen, afterwards chosen chairman of the committee of arrangements for the present council, voiced informally the desire of the Americans to reciprocate the hospitalities so generously extended, and action finally crystallized in the appointment of a committee of fifteen, representing the British Isles, America, and the colonies, to take the necessary initial steps.

On this side of the water the matter was first broached at the meeting of the National Council in Minneapolis in 1892. Three years later, at the National Council of 1895 held in Syracuse, a committee of thirty ministers and laymen was appointed to make the preliminary arrangements. From this larger committee a sub-committee of eleven was chosen as a working executive force, and out of that a program committee.

GENERAL COMMITTEE OF ARRANGEMENTS

Appointed by the

NATIONAL COUNCIL.

(The first eleven on the list constitute the Executive Committee.)

SAMUEL B. CAPEN, Massachusetts.
Rev. ARTHUR LITTLE, D.D., Massachusetts.
Rev. HENRY A. HAZEN, D.D., Massachusetts.
Rev. ALBERT E. DUNNING, D.D., Massachusetts.
G. HENRY WHITCOMB, Massachusetts.
Rev. HENRY A. STIMSON, D.D., New York.
Rev. AMORY H. BRADFORD, D.D., New Jersey.
Rev. GEORGE A. GORDON, D.D., Massachusetts.
Rev. PHILIP S. MOXOM, D.D., Massachusetts.
Rev. WILLIAM H. MOORE, Connecticut.
ROWLAND G. HAZARD, Rhode Island.

CYRUS NORTHROP, Minnesota.
Rev. FREDERICK A. NOBLE, D.D., Illinois.
Rev. JOHN K. MCLEAN, D.D., California.
Rev. CHARLES H. RICHARDS, D.D., Pennsylvania.
HENRY C. ROBINSON, Connecticut.
Rev. WASHINGTON GLADDEN, D.D., Ohio.
Rev. ROBERT R. MEREDITH, D.D., New York.
Rev. WILLIAM F. SLOCUM, D.D., Colorado.
Rev. EDWARD D. EATON, D.D., Wisconsin.
Rev. THEODORE T. MUNGER, D.D., Connecticut.
ELIPHALET W. BLATCHFORD, Illinois.
Rev. SIDNEY STRONG, D.D., Illinois.
Justice DAVID J. BREWER, District of Columbia.
Rev. WILLIAM H. DAVIS, D.D., Massachusetts.
NATHAN P. DODGE, Iowa.
Rev. WILLIAM E. GRIFFIS, D.D., New York.
Rev. MICHAEL BURNHAM, D.D., Missouri.

Program Committee.

Rev. GEORGE A. GORDON, D.D.

Rev. A. H. BRADFORD, D.D.   Rev. ARTHUR LITTLE, D.D.
Rev. A. E. DUNNING, D.D.   Rev. P. S. MOXOM, D.D.

Rev. H. A. HAZEN, D.D.

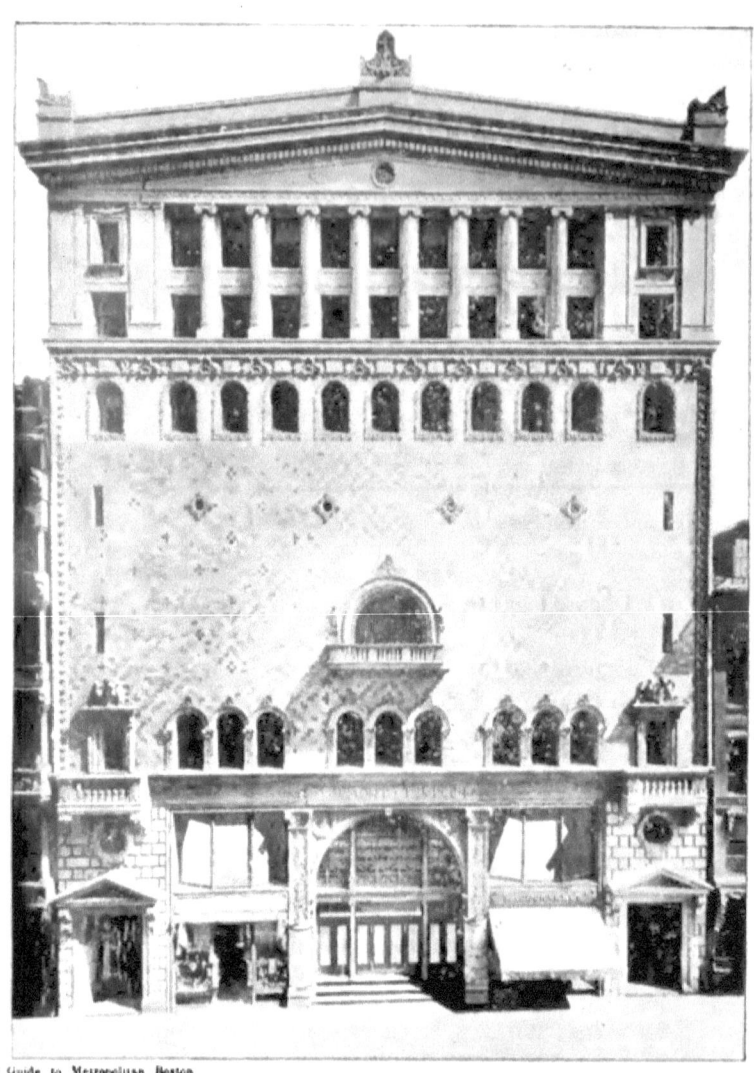

TREMONT TEMPLE.

Place of Meeting of the International Council.

JAMES BURRILL ANGELL, LL.D.
President of the International Council.

HIS EXCELLENCY GOV. ROGER WOLCOTT, LL.D.
HIS HONOR MAYOR JOSIAH QUINCY.

ANDREW MARTIN FAIRBAIRN, D.D., L.L.D.
Preacher of the International Council.

Program

International Congregational Council,

September 20-28, 1899.

Place of Meeting, Tremont Temple.
Possible overflow meetings in Park Street Church.

Wednesday, September 20.

AFTERNOON.

Organization.
Address of welcome in behalf of the Committee of Arrangements by Samuel Billings Capen, M.A., Chairman.
Roll Call.

EVENING.

Addresses of Welcome.
His Excellency the Governor of the Commonwealth, Roger Wolcott, LL.D.
His Honor the Mayor of the City of Boston, Josiah Quincy.

President's Address.
James Burrill Angell, LL.D., President of the University of Michigan, Ann Arbor, Mich.

Thursday, September 21.

FORENOON.

Fundamental Principles in Theology.
George Harris, D.D., LL.D., President elect of Amherst College, Amherst, Mass.

Message of the Old Testament for To-day.
Frank Chamberlain Porter, D.D., Ph.D., Winkley Professor of Biblical Theology at Yale University, New Haven, Conn.

Program

AFTERNOON.

The Historical Method in Theology.
George Park Fisher, D.D., LL.D., Titus Street Professor of Ecclesiastical History and Dean of the Divinity School, Yale University, New Haven, Conn.

Theology the Order of Nature.
Rev. Alexander Gosman, Principal and Professor of New Testament Exegesis, Theology, Apologetics, and Homiletics at the Congregational College of Victoria, Hawthorn, Australia, and Pastor of the Congregational Church in Hawthorn.

The Evangelical Principle of Authority.
Peter Taylor Forsyth, M.A., D.D., Pastor of Emmanuel Church, Cambridge, England.

EVENING.

Sermon.
Andrew Martin Fairbairn, D.D., LL.D., Principal of Mansfield College, Oxford, England.

Friday, September 22.

FORENOON.

The Christian Idea of the State.
Joseph Compton Rickett, D.L., M.P., Scarborough, England.

Municipal Government as a Sphere for the Christian Man.
William Crosfield, Esq., J.P., Treasurer of the Congregational Union of England and Wales, Liverpool, England.
Samuel Billings Capen, M.A., Boston, Mass.

At 12.30, *RECEPTION* at the Vendome, corner Commonwealth Avenue and Dartmouth Street.

EVENING.

Distinctive Characteristics of Christianity.
Charles Reynolds Brown, D.D., Pastor of First Church, Oakland, Cal.
Rev. John Daniel Jones, M.A., B.D., Pastor of the Richmond Hill Congregational Church, Bournemouth, England.

The Influence of the Study of Other Religions upon Christian Theology.
Andrew Martin Fairbairn, D.D., LL.D., Principal of Mansfield College, Oxford, England.

Program

Saturday, September 23.

FORENOON.

The Church in Social Reforms.

Albert Spicer, Esq., M.P., London, England.

Graham Taylor, D.D., LL.D., Professor of Christian Sociology and Pastoral Theology at Chicago Theological Seminary, Chicago, Ill.

AFTERNOON.

An *EXCURSION* to Salem.

Sunday, September 24.

FORENOON.

No session.

AFTERNOON.

Lord's Supper at the Old South Church, Copley Square, corner Boylston and Dartmouth Streets.

Monday, September 25.

FORENOON.

Tendencies of Modern Education.

John Massie, M.A., J.P., Yates Professor of New Testament Exegesis at Mansfield College, Oxford, England.

Rev. James Hirst Hollowell, Rochdale, England, Secretary of the Nonconformist Political Council of Great Britain, and of the Northern Counties Education League.

AFTERNOON.

The Influence of our Public Schools on the Caste Spirit.

Frederick Alphonso Noble, D.D., Pastor of the Union Park Church, Chicago, Ill.

Ll. D. Bevan, LL.B., D.D., Professor of Old Testament Exegesis and Church History at the Congregational College of Victoria, Melbourne, Australia, and Pastor of the Queensberry Street Congregational Church, Melbourne.

The Religious Motive in Education as Illustrated in the History of American Colleges.

William Jewett Tucker, D.D., LL.D., President of Dartmouth College, Hanover, N. H.

Program

EVENING.
> Addresses by
>> Charles William Eliot, LL.D., President of Harvard University, Cambridge, Mass.
>> William DeWitt Hyde, D.D., LL.D., President of Bowdoin College, Brunswick, Me.
>> William Frederick Slocum, B.D., LL.D., President of Colorado College, Colorado Springs, Col.
>> Henry Hopkins, D.D., Pastor of First Church, Kansas City, Mo.

Tuesday, September 26.

FORENOON.
> *The Pastoral Function, Congregational and Civic.*
>> Rev. William Boothby Selbie, M.A., Pastor of Highgate Congregational Church, London, England.
>> Reuen Thomas, D.D., Pastor of Harvard Church, Brookline, Mass.
>
> *The Spiritual Life in our Churches.*
>> Rev. Joseph Robertson, M.A., Pastor of Stow Memorial Church, Adelaide, Australia, and Principal of the Congregational College of South Australia.

AFTERNOON.
> *Woman's Work.*
>> Mrs. Elkanah Armitage, Leeds, England.
>> Miss Margaret J. Evans, A.M., Professor of English Literature and Modern Languages at Carleton College, Northfield, Minn.
>
> *Woman's Work in Foreign Missions.*
>> Grace Niebuhr Kimball, M.D., Assistant Physician at Vassar College, Poughkeepsie, N. Y.

EVENING.
> *The Young People.*
>> Cornelius Howard Patton, D.D., Pastor of the First Church, St. Louis, Mo.
>> Charles Edward Jefferson, D.D., Pastor of Broadway Tabernacle Church, New York, N. Y.
>> Rev. Charles Silvester Horne, M.A., Pastor of Kensington Congregational Church, London.

Program

Wednesday, September 27.

FORENOON.

Obligations and Opportunities of Congregationalism.

In Great Britain: Robert Bruce, M.A., D.D., Pastor of Highfield Congregational Church, Huddersfield, England.

In America: Williston Walker, Ph.D., D.D., Professor of Germanic and Western Church History, on the Waldo Foundation, at Hartford Theological Seminary, Hartford, Conn.

In Victoria: Rev. Jacob John Halley, Pastor of St. Kilda Congregational Church, Melbourne, Victoria, and Secretary of the Victorian Congregational Union.

In other countries: Speakers to be named.

Scottish Congregationalism: James Stark, D.D., Pastor of the Belmont Street Congregational Church, Aberdeen, Scotland.

AFTERNOON.

Independence and Fellowship.

Albert Josiah Lyman, D.D., Pastor of the South Congregational Church, Brooklyn, N. Y.

John Brown, D.D., Pastor of the Bunyan Meeting, Bedford, England.

Duty of the Stronger to the Weaker Churches.

Rev. Henry Arnold Thomas, M.A., Chairman of the Congregational Union of England and Wales, Bristol, England.

EVENING.

RECEPTION by the Congregational Club.

Greetings from Other Denominations.

William Lawrence, D.D., S.T.D., Protestant Episcopal Bishop of Massachusetts.

Augustus Hopkins Strong, D.D., LL.D., President of Rochester Theological Seminary and Professor of Theology, Rochester, N. Y.

Charles Cuthbert Hall, D.D., President of Union Theological Seminary, New York, N. Y.

William Fairfield Warren, LL.D., President Boston University, Boston, Mass.

Francis Greenwood Peabody, A.M., D.D., Plummer Professor of Christian Morals, and Parkman Professor of Theology at Harvard University, Cambridge, Mass.

Program

Thursday, September 28.

FORENOON.

International Relations and Responsibilities.
Lyman Abbott, D.D., Editor of *The Outlook*, New York, N. Y.

The Christian Attitude towards War in the Light of Recent Events.
Alexander Mackennal, D.D., Pastor at Bowdon, England.

AFTERNOON.

Adaptation of Methods to New Conditions in Foreign Missions.
Rev. Ralph Wardlaw Thompson, Senior Foreign Secretary of the London Missionary Society, London.

The Permanent Motive in Missionary Work.
Richard Salter Storrs, D.D., LL.D., Pastor of Church of The Pilgrims, Brooklyn, N. Y., and former President of the American Board of Commissioners for Foreign Missions.

EVENING.

The Living Christ.
Alfred Cave, D.D., Principal and Professor of Theological Encyclopædia, Apologetics, Doctrinal Theology, and Homiletics, at Hackney College, London, England.

The Holy Spirit in the Churches.
Frank Wakeley Gunsaulus, D.D., Pastor of Central Church (Independent), Chicago, and President of Armour Institute.

Friday, September 29.

An *EXCURSION* to Plymouth.

DELEGATES TO THE INTERNATIONAL COUNCIL

UNITED STATES.

Abbott, Rev. Lyman, Brooklyn, N. Y.
Ackerman, Rev. Arthur W., Portland, Ore.
Adams, Rev. Ephraim, Waterloo, Io.
Ainslie, Rev. James S., Ft. Wayne, Ind.
Angell, Pres. James B., Ann Arbor, Mich.
Bailey, Rev. Amos J., Seattle, Wash.
Bailey, Rev. Henry L., Middletown Springs, Vt.
Baldwin, Simeon E., New Haven, Conn.
Barrows, Rev. John H., Oberlin, O.
Barton, Rev. William E., Oak Park, Ill.
Bell, Judge Charles W., Lawrence, Mass.
Bell, David C., Minneapolis, Minn.
Blatchford, Eliphalet W., Chicago, Ill.
Borden, Col. Thomas, Fall River, Mass.
Boynton, Rev. Nehemiah, Detroit, Mich.
Bradford, Rev. Amory H., Montclair, N. J.
Bradley, Rev. Dan F., Grand Rapids, Mich.
Bradley, Pres. John E., Jacksonville, Ill.
Bradshaw, Rev. John W., Ann Arbor, Mich.
Brainerd, Pres. E., Middlebury, Vt.
Brewster, John L., Andover, Mass.
Bross, Rev. Harmon, Lincoln, Neb.
Brown, Rev. Amasa A., Hot Springs, So. Dak.
Brown, Rev. Charles R., Oakland, Cal.
Brown, Rev. Clarence T., Salt Lake City, Utah.
Buckham, Pres. Matthew H., Burlington, Vt.
Burnham, Rev. Michael, St. Louis, Mo.
Bushnell, Rev. Albert, St. Joseph, Mo.
Buss, Rev. William H., Fremont, Neb.
Came, Samuel M., Alfred, Me.
Campbell, Rev. James M., Lombard, Ill.
Capen, Samuel B., Boston, Mass.
Carroll, Rev. W. Irving, Dallas, Tex.
Carter, Pres. Franklin, Williamstown, Mass.
Champlin, Rev. Oliver P., Dwight, No. Dak.
Clarke, Rev. Almon T., Shelby, Ala.
Clark, Rev. DeWitt S., Salem, Mass.
Clark, Rev. Francis E., Auburndale, Mass.
Clark, Rev. William D., Billings, Mont.
Cobb, Rev. L. Henry, New York, N. Y.
Coffin, Hon. O. Vincent, Middletown, Conn.
Conant, Edward, Randolph Center, Vt.
Cooper, Rev. James W., New Britain, Conn.

Delegates to the International Council

Crane, Hon. W. Murray, Dalton, Mass.
Cravath, Rev. Pres. Erastus M., Nashville, Tenn.
Crawford, Rev. William, Sparta, Wis.
Danforth, Rev. James R., Westfield, N. J.
Davis, Rev. David L., Williamstown, Penn.
Davis, Rev. William H., Newton, Mass.
Demond, Rev. Abraham L., Montgomery, Ala.
De Peu, Rev. John, Bridgeport, Conn.
Dexter, Rev. Morton, Boston, Mass.
Dickinson, Rev. C. H., Canandaigua, N. Y.
Doane, Rev. John, Lincoln, Neb.
Dodge, Nathan P., Council Bluffs, Io.
Dudley, Guilford, Poughkeepsie, N. Y.
Dunning, Rev. Albert E., Boston, Mass.
Eaton, Rev. Pres. Edward D., Beloit, Wis.
Eggert, Mrs. Frederick, Portland, Ore.
Evans, W. D., Hampton, Io.
Evans, Miss Margaret J., Northfield, Minn.
Fairbanks, Rev. Henry, St. Johnsbury, Vt.
Fairchild, Rev. George T., Berea, Ky.
Fisher, Rev. George P., New Haven, Conn.
Fitch, Rev. Franklin S., Buffalo, N. Y.
Forbes, Rev. Samuel B., Hartford, Conn.
Ford, H. Clark, Cleveland, O.
Fraser, Rev. John G., Cleveland, O.
Frisbie, Rev. Alvah L., Des Moines, Io.
Gilbert, Deacon Lewis N., Ware, Mass.
Gist, Rev. William W., Osage, Io.
Gladden, Rev. Washington, Columbus, O.
Gordon, Rev. George A., Boston, Mass.
Griffis, Rev. William E., Ithaca, N. Y.
Gunsaulus, Rev. F. W., Chicago, Ill.
Haines, Hon. R. M., Grinnell, Io.
Hall, Rev. George E., Dover, N. H.
Hallock, Rev. Leavitt H., Minneapolis, Minn.
Harris, Rev. George, Andover, Mass.
Hart, Prin. Alexis C., Franklin, Neb.
Hawes, Rev. Edward, Burlington, Vt.
Hawkes, Rev. Winfield S., Springfield, Mass.
Hayes, Rev. Francis L., Manitou, Col.
Hazard, Rowland G., Peacedale, R. I.
Hazen, Rev. Azel W., Middletown, Conn.
Hazen, Rev. Henry A., Auburndale, Mass.
Henderson, Rev. George W., New Orleans, La.
Herrick, Rev. Samuel E., Boston, Mass.
Hill, Rev. Jesse, Wakeman, O.
Hobbs, Rev. William A., Warsaw, N. Y.
Hollister, Harvey J., Grand Rapids, Mich.
Hollister, Dr. John H., Chicago, Ill.

Delegates to the International Council

Holway, Oscar, Augusta, Me.
Hopkins, Charles A., Brookline, Mass.
Hopkins, Rev. Henry, Kansas City, Mo.
Howard, Gen. Charles H., Chicago, Ill.
Hyde, Rev. Albert M., Toledo, O.
Hyde, Rev. Nathaniel A., Indianapolis, Ind.
Hyde, Rev. Pres. William D., Brunswick, Me.
James, Rev. D. Melancthon, Plymouth, Mass.
James, Rev. Horace P., Colfax, Wash.
Jefferson, Rev. Charles E., New York, N. Y.
Jenkins, Rev. Frank E., Atlanta, Ga.
Jernberg, Rev. R. A., Chicago, Ill.
Jones, Rev. Rees S., Scranton, Penn.
Kimball, Dr. Grace, Poughkeepsie, N. Y.
Kloss, Rev. Daniel, Tempe, Ariz.
Knodell, Rev. James R., Oakland, Cal.
Kyle, James H., Aberdeen, So. Dak.
Lewis, Rev. George, South Berwick, Me.
Little, Rev. Arthur, Boston, Mass.
Loba, Rev. Jean F., Evanston, Ill.
Loomis, Dwight, Hartford, Conn.
Lyman, Rev. Albert J., Brooklyn, N. Y.
McClelland, Rev. Pres. Thomas, Forest Grove, Ore.
McCully, Rev. Charles G., Calais, Me.
McLean, Rev. John K., Oakland, Cal.
McMillan, Hon. T. C., Chicago, Ill.
Maxwell, Rev. Leigh B., Decatur, Ga.
Meredith, Rev. R. R., Brooklyn, N. Y.
Mills, Rev. Charles S., Cleveland, O.
Miner, Rev. Henry A., Madison, Wis.
Moody, Dwight L., Northfield, Mass.
Moore, Rev. William H., Hartford, Conn.
Moses, Galen C., Bath, Me.
Moxom, Rev. Philip S., Springfield, Mass.
Munger, Rev. Theodore T., New Haven, Conn.
Newman, Rev. Stephen M., Washington, D. C.
Nichols, Rev. John R., Marietta, O.
Noble, Rev. F. A., Chicago, Ill.
Noble, Rev. Mason, Lake Helen, Fla.
Nutting, Rev. Wallace, Providence, R. I.
Osgood, Charles W., Bellows Falls, Vt.
Osterhout, William H., Ridgeway, Pa.
Packard, Rev. Edward N., Syracuse, N. Y.
Park, Rev. William E., Gloversville, N. Y.
Parker, Rev. Edwin P., Hartford, Conn.
Parker, Rev. J. Homer, Kingfisher, Okl.
Patton, Rev. Cornelius H., St. Louis, Mo.
Perry, John E., Southport, Conn.
Pitkin, E. H., Chicago, Ill.

Delegates to the International Council

Plumb, Rev. Albert H., Boston, Mass.
Porter, Rev. Prof. Frank C., New Haven, Conn.
Pound, Rev. William H., Cortland, N. Y.
Pratt, Rev. Lewellyn, Norwich, Conn.
Ragland, Rev. Fountain G., Wilmington, N. C.
Richards, Rev. Charles H., Philadelphia, Penn.
Richardson, Rev. Cyrus, Nashua, N. H.
Robinson, Henry C., Hartford, Conn.
Robinson, Rev. William A., Middletown, N. Y.
Rowland, Rev. Lyman S., Lee, Mass.
Salter, Rev. William, Burlington, Io.
Savage, Rev. George S. F., Chicago, Ill.
Scott, Rev. Prof. Hugh M., Chicago, Ill.
Simpkin, Rev. Peter A., Gallup, N. M.
Slocum, Rev. Pres. William F., Colorado Springs, Col.
Smith, Rev. Judson, Boston, Mass.
Smith, Lyndon A., Montevideo, Minn.
Smith, Nicholas, Milwaukee, Wis.
Smyth, Rev. Newman, New Haven, Conn.
Stearns, Richard H., Boston, Mass.
Stevens, Rev. Prof. George B., New Haven, Conn.
Stimson, Rev. Henry A., New York, N. Y.
Storrs, Rev. R. S., Brooklyn, N. Y.
Stowell, C. B., Hudson, Mich.
Strong, Rev. Pres. James W., Northfield, Minn.
Strong, Rev. Sydney, Oak Park, Ill.
Strong, William H., Detroit, Mich.
Sutherland, Rev. Ward T., Oxford, N. Y.
Taft, Dr. Jonathan, Cincinnati, O.
Taintor, Rev. Jesse F., Rochester, Minn.
Taylor, Rev. Graham, Chicago, Ill.
Tenney, Rev. Henry M., Oberlin, O.
Tewksbury, Rev. George A., Concord, Mass.
Thain, Rev. Alexander R., Chicago, Ill.
Thomas, Rev. Reuen, Brookline, Mass.
Thrall, Rev. W. Herbert, Huron, So. Dak.
Tucker, Edwin, Eureka, Kan.
Tucker, Rev. Pres. William J., Hanover, N. H.
Tunnell, Rev. Robert M., Manhattan, Kan.
Vose, Rev. James G., Providence, R. I.
Walker, Prof. Williston, Hartford, Conn.
Wanamaker, William H., Philadelphia, Penn.
Ward, Rev. William H., New York, N. Y.
Warner, Lucien C., New York, N. Y.
Wellman, Arthur H., Malden, Mass.
Welles, Rev. T. Clayton, Taunton, Mass.
Whitcomb, G. Henry, Worcester, Mass.
Whitehead, John M., Janesville, Wis.
Whitelaw, Oscar L., St. Louis, Mo.

Delegates to the International Council

Williston, A. Lyman, Northampton, Mass.
Woodworth, Edward B., Concord, N. H.
Woodworth, Rev. Pres. Frank G., Tougaloo, Miss.
Wright, E. L., Hancock, Mich.

GREAT BRITAIN.

Ainslie, Rev. William J., Greenock.
Anstey, Rev. Martin, Dewsbury.
Armitage, Rev. Prof. Elkanah, Leeds.
Armitage, Mrs. Elkanah, Leeds.
Baines, G. H., West Hartlepool.
Baines, Alexander, Leicester.
Baker, Rev. J. Kitto, Rochester.
Bartlet, Rev. Prof. J. Vernon, Oxford.
Bolton, Rev. William, London.
Bridge, Rev. Arthur G., London.
Brindley, Rev. Richard B., Nottingham.
Brown, Rev. John, Bedford.
Bruce, Rev. Robert, Huddersfield.
Cave, Rev. Prin. Alfred, London.
Chapple, Rev. G. Porter, Melbourn, Royston.
Cheetham, Miss, London.
Clarke, James G., London.
Cleland, W. W., Belfast, Ireland.
Cooper, Rev. Joseph J., Northampton.
Coutts, James, Edinburgh.
Cowper-Smith, Rev. George W., Tunbridge Wells.
Craig, Rev. Robert, Edinburgh.
Crosfield, William, Liverpool.
Dale, Rev. Bryan, Bradford.
Darby, Rev. William E., London.
Davies, Rev. Henry A., Aberdare, Wales.
Davison, Rev. William H., Edinburgh.
Dowsett, Thomas, Essex.
Dryerre, Rev. John M., Manchester.
Easterbrook, Rev. John C., Somerton.
Fairbairn, Rev. Prin. Andrew M., Oxford.
Fitch, F. G., London.
Flower, Rev. James E., London.
Forsyth, Rev. Peter T., Cambridge.
Goddard, D. Ford, M.P., Ipswich.

Delegates to the International Council

Hamilton, Rev. Edward, Southend.
Harrison, Thomas W., Hanley, Staffordshire.
Hastings, Rev. Frederick, London.
Hawkins, F. H. Wrexham, Wales.
Hewgill, Rev. William, Farnworth.
Hollowell, Rev. J. Hirst, Rochdale.
Hooke, Rev. D. Burford, London.
Hooke, Mrs. D. Burford, London.
Hooper, A. G., Dudley.
Horne, Rev. C. Silvester, London.
Irons, Rev. David E., Glasgow.
Johnson, Rev. Arthur N., London.
Johnstone, Rev. Thomas, Dundee.
Jones, G. O., Liverpool.
Jones, Rev. John D., Bournemouth.
Jones, Rev. J. Gwilym, Penarth, Wales.
Jones, Rev. Morgan, Bolton, Lancashire.
Jones, Rev. W. Ivor, Swansea, Wales.
Lansdown, Rev. Francis, Leicester.
Lansdown, Rev. Matthias, London.
Lee, Henry, Manchester.
Lee, Rev. William L., Kettering.
Leith, John, Aberdeen, Scot.
Lester, E. R., Plymouth.
Link, Charles W., Croydon, Surry.
Macfadyen, Rev. Dugold, Hanley, Stafford.
Mackennal, Rev. Alexander, Bowdon.
Mann, Rev. Edgar, Port Guernsey.
Martin, Rev. G. Currie, Reigate.
Massie, Prof. John, Oxford.
Meggitt, J. C., Barry, Wales.
Meserve, Rev. Isaac C., London.
Morgan, A. F., Leamington.
Morgan, Rev. G. Campbell, London.
Newsum, Henry, Lincoln.
Norbury, J. C., Manchester.
Ogle, Rev. Joseph, Sherborne.
Parry, Edward, Nottingham.
Patrick, Rev. John A., Manchester.
Powell, Rev. Edward P., Rock Ferry.
Poynter, Rev. John J., Oswestry.
Rees, Rev. J. Machreth, London.
Reeve, T. F., Ware, Herts.
Ricketts, J. Compton, M.P., London.
Ritchie, Rev. David L., Newcastle-on-Tyne.
Rowland, Rev. Alfred, London.
Sandison, Rev. Alexander, London.
Sargeant, Alfred R., Brighton.
Scott, Rev. Prin. Caleb A., Manchester.

Delegates to the International Council

Selbie, Rev. William B., London.
Shepheard, A. J., London.
Simpson, Rev. Prof. Andrew F., Portobello.
Smith, D. S., Dundee.
Smith, Edward, Bewdley.
Smith, Rev. Norman H., Oxford.
Snow, A. D., Worthing, Sussex.
Spicer, Albert, M.P., London.
Spicer, Evan, London.
Stancliff, Charles, London.
Stark, Rev. James, Aberdeen.
Stephens, Rev. J. Hale, Chepstow.
Stewart, Halley, M.P., London.
Styles, James, Warwick.
Tatton, Rev. Dan, Hemel, Hempstead.
Tavender, Rev. Frederick, Great Marlow.
Thomas, Rev. H. Arnold, Bristol.
Thomas, Miss Rotha, Bristol.
Thomas, Rev. Owen, London.
Thompson, Rev. R. Wardlaw, London.
Titchmarsh, Rev. Edward H., Newbury.
Toms, C. B., London.
Toms, C. W., London.
Toms, Rev. Henry S., London.
Townsend, Rev. Thomas, Shrewsbury.
Turner, Rev. Horace W., Bolton.
Veitch, Rev. Robert, Liverpool.
Wells, Rev. Richard J., Stonecroft, Havant.
Wilkins, Prof. A. S., Manchester.
Wilkinson, J. Rennie, Addington, Thrapston.
Willis, Mark, Sheffield.
Wills, Rev. John, London.
Wilson, Rev. Alexander, Bristol.
Woods, Rev. William J., London.
Wylie, Rev. James, Belfast.

BRITISH NORTH AMERICA.

Austin, Rev. James M., Sheffield Academy, N. B.
Ball, Rev. George W., Liverpool, N. S.
Braithwaite, Rev. Edward E., Yarmouth, N. S.
Chancey, L. T., St. Johns, Newfoundland.
Cox, Rev. Jacob W., Lower Selmah, N. S.
Cushing, Charles, Montreal, Que.
Dougall, J. R., Montreal, Que.
Duff, Rev. Charles, Brooklyn, N. S.
Duff, J. M. M., Montreal, Que.
Duley, F. J., St. Johns, Newfoundland.
George, Rev. Prin. J. H., Montreal, Que.

Delegates to the International Council

Gerrie, Rev. John P., Toronto, Ont.
Gurd, Charles, Montreal, Que.
Hall, Rev. Thomas, Melbourne, Que.
Hill, Rev. Edward M., Montreal, Que.
Hyde, Mrs. T. B., Toronto, Ont.
Minchin, Rev. William J., St. John, N. B.
Morton, Rev. John, Hamilton, Ont.
O'Hara, Henry, Toronto, Ont.
Scholfield, Rev. John, Brantford, Ont.
Silcox, Rev. E. D., Paris, Ont.
Thackeray, Rev. Joseph, St. Johns, Newfoundland.
Warriner, Prof. W. Henry, Montreal, Que.
Whiteley, W. H., St. Johns, Newfoundland.
Wood, Rev. Morgan, Toronto, Ont.
Yeigh, Edward.

AUSTRALIA.

Bell, George, Kew.
Bevan, Rev. Llewellyn D., Melbourne.
Bevan, Penry Vaughan, Melbourne.
Cockhead, Leslie G., New Town, Tasmania.
Fowlds, George, Auckland, New Zealand.
Gosman, Rev. Prof. Alexander, Hawthorn.
Griffith, Rev. A. J., M. A., Waverley, Sydney.
Halley, Rev. J. John, Melbourne.
Halsey, William, Melbourne.
Lewis, Rev. William H., Ballarat.
Rickard, Rev. James, Brighton.
Robertson, Rev. Joseph, Adelaide.
Saunders, Rev. William, Dunedin, New Zealand.
Toms, Rev. J. Henwood, S. Brisbane, Queensland.
Woodhill, A. M., Burwood, Sydney.

JAPAN.

Cary, Rev. Otis.
Miyagawa, Rev. Tsunetern, Osaka.

HAWAII.

Desha, Rev. Stephen L., Hilo.
Emerson, Rev. Oliver P., Honolulu.
Ezera, Rev. J. M., Ewa, Oahu.
Hyde, Charles M., Honolulu.
Kauhane, Rev. J., Waiohinu.
Timoteo, Rev. E. S., Honolulu.
Waterhouse, Henry, Honolulu.

AFRICA.

Dower, Rev. William, Port Elizabeth, Cape Colony.
Forbes, Rev. William, S. Africa.
Pixley, Rev. Stephen C., Inanda.
Pritchard, Rev. James, Port Elizabeth, Cape Colony.

Delegates to the International Council

ASIA.

Dwight, Rev. Henry O., Constantinople.
Fairbank, Rev. Henry, Wadale, India.
Lee, Rev. Lucius O., Marash, Turkey.
Sheffield, Rev. Devello Z., Tung-cho, China.
Smith, Rev. Thomas S., Tillapally, India.

MICRONESIA.

Price, Rev. Frank M., Ruk.

MEXICO.

Eaton, Rev. James D., Chihuahua.

Pilgrim Sight-seer's Directory

THE PUBLIC LIBRARY is on Copley Square, near Trinity Church. All departments of the library are open every week day from 9 A.M. to 9 P.M., and on Sundays from 2 to 9 P.M. The mural decorations of Puvis de Chavannes, E. A. Abbey, John S. Sargent, and the special collections of this library, notably the eighteenth-century library of Rev. Thomas Prince, of Boston, are worth careful study.

MUSEUM OF NATURAL HISTORY. — Cor. Boylston and Berkeley Streets. Open Wednesdays and Saturdays, 10 to 5. Free. Other week days, 9 to 5. Fee 25 cents.

MUSEUM OF FINE ARTS. — Copley Square and Dartmouth Street. 9 to 5. Fee 25 cents. Sundays 1 to 5. Saturdays and Sundays free.

CENTRAL CHURCH, Congregational, cor. Newbury and Berkeley Streets, Back Bay District, is notable for its stained glass and artistic decoration. It is open every afternoon, save Saturday, from 1 to 3 P.M.

THE OLD SOUTH CHURCH, cor. Boylston and Dartmouth Streets, Copley Square, has memorial tablets to Samuel Adams and eminent divines, and is open daily in the afternoon.

TRINITY CHURCH, Copley Square, designed by Richardson, former church of Phillips Brooks. Open daily.

GENEALOGICAL ROOMS. — 18 Somerset Street. New England History and Genealogy. 9 to 5. Saturdays to 2. Free.

OLD SOUTH. — Corner Washington and Milk Streets. Loan Historic Collection of Relics and Pictures, etc. 9 to 6. Fee 25 cents.

BOSTONIAN SOCIETY'S ROOMS. — Old State House, head of State Street. Memorial Halls and Historic Collections. 9.30 to 5. Free.

FANEUIL HALL. — Merchants' Row and Faneuil Hall Square. Historic Paintings. 9 to 4. Free.

STATE HOUSE. — Beacon, head of Park Street. Statuary, Battle Flags, War Relics, etc. 8 to 5. Free.

CHRIST CHURCH is on Salem Street in the North End of the city. It is the oldest church building now standing in the city.

BUNKER HILL MONUMENT. — Monument Square, Charlestown. Revolutionary Relics, etc. 8 to 6. Fee 20 cents.

PEABODY MUSEUM. — Divinity Avenue, Cambridge. American and Foreign Archæology and Ethnology. 9 to 5. Closed holidays. Free.

WARE COLLECTION of Blaschka Glass Models of Plants and Flowers. Central section of University Museum, Cambridge. Entrance Oxford Street. 9 to 4. Free. Open Sundays. 1 to 5.

AGASSIZ MUSEUM. — Divinity Avenue, Cambridge. Comparative Zoological and Botanical Collections. 9 to 5. Free. Open Sundays. 1 to 5.

BOSTON ON THE CHARLES.

PART III

Additional Illustrations

...AND...

Business Information

Foreword to Part III

*T*HE *following pages are intended to supplement and complete Parts I and II of this book in two ways. First, by supplying a number of interesting illustrations which could not be placed in connection with the preceding text to good advantage; second, by offering to those who use* THE BOSTON BOOK *a compact business directory.*

The firms and individuals represented in the following pages are of the first rank in their respective lines, and may be consulted with absolute confidence. It was the intention of the publishers of this book to secure a characteristic representation of businesses which supply the needs of our churches and of individuals interested in them and in their history and literature. The hearty co-operation of nearly forty has insured the completeness and value of this part of THE BOSTON BOOK *beyond the expectations of its publishers.*

W. L. GREENE & CO.,
Proprietors of The Congregationalist,
14 Beacon Street, Boston, Mass., U.S.A.

Index to Business Information

	PAGE
Andover Publications, W. F. Draper	197
AUSTIN ORGAN CO., Pipe Organs	219
BARTLETT, N. J. & CO., Booksellers	179
Bells, Meneely Bell Co.	213
"Beacon Biographies," Small, Maynard & Co.	191
BIBLE STUDY PUBLISHING CO., Sunday-school Lessons	207
Bibles, Oxford University Press	205
Blakeslee Sunday-school Lessons, Bible Study Publishing Co.	207

Bookstores.
- N. J. Bartlett & Co., Theological and General. Choice Editions ... 179
- Damrell & Upham, "Old Corner Bookstore" ... 180
- Little, Brown & Co. ... 183
- Burbank's Pilgrim Bookstore ... 203

Boston Guide. Mr. F. A. Waterman	177
BURBANK'S PILGRIM BOOKSTORE, Plymouth	203
"Bushnell, Horace," Life by Rev. T. T. Munger	185
Byington, Rev. E. H., Books by	183
Carpets, Torrey, Bright & Capen Company	171
CENTURY CO., THE, Publishers (Fourth cover page.)	
Communion Cups, Individual, Reed & Barton	217
CONGREGATIONALIST, THE	5

Church Equipment.
- Bells, Meneely Bell Co. ... 213
- Carpets, Torrey, Bright & Capen Company ... 171
- Communion Cups, Reed & Barton ... 217
- Glass and Decoration, Tiffany Glass & Decorating Co. ... 211
- Hymn Books, The Century Co. ... (Fourth cover page.)
- Lights, Wheeler Reflector Co. ... 215
- Organs, Austin Organ Co. ... 219

DAMRELL & UPHAM, Booksellers	180
DRAPER, W. F., Publisher	197

Dry Goods and Department Stores.
- Gilchrist & Co. ... 167
- Houghton & Dutton ... 232
- C. F. Hovey & Co. ... 169
- Shepard, Norwell & Co. ... (Third cover page.)

Education.
- New England Conservatory of Music ... 223
- Wheaton Seminary, Norton, Mass. ... 225

GAZE, H. & SONS, Travel	6
GILCHRIST & CO., Dry Goods	167
Gordon, Rev. George A., Books by	189
GREENE, W. L. & CO., The Congregationalist, Books, Services	5, 181, 221
Guide Books, George H. Walker & Co.	227
Historic China, Jones, McDuffee & Stratton Company	173
"Historic Pilgrimages in New England"	193
HOUGHTON & DUTTON, Department Store	232
HOUGHTON, MIFFLIN & CO., Publishers	185, 187, 189
HOVEY, C. F. & CO., Dry Goods	169
Hymn Books, "In Excelsis," The Century Co. (Fourth cover page.)	
JONES, McDUFFEE & STRATTON COMPANY, Historic China	173
Lights, Wheeler Reflector Co.	215
LITTLE, BROWN & CO., Publishers	183
LOTHROP PUBLISHING COMPANY, Publishers	195

Maps.
- Damrell & Upham ... 180
- George H. Walker & Co. ... 227

McKenzie, Rev. Alexander, Books by	187
MENEELY BELL CO., Church Bells	213
MERRIAM, G. & C. COMPANY, Dictionaries	199
Munger, Rev. T. T., Life of Bushnell, by	185

Index to Business Information

	PAGE
NEW ENGLAND CONSERVATORY OF MUSIC	223
NEW ENGLAND MAGAZINE, Warren F. Kellogg, Publisher. (Second cover.)	
Old Corner Bookstore	180
Organs, Austin Organ Co.	219
OXFORD UNIVERSITY PRESS, Bibles	205
Peloubet's Sunday-school Lessons and Select Notes	209
Periodicals.	
Blakeslee's Quarterlies	207
The Congregationalist	5
New England Magazine (Second cover.)	
Peloubet's Quarterlies	209
The Youth's Companion	201
Periodicals sold at the "Old Corner Bookstore"	180
Photographic Views, Soule Photograph Co.	175
Plymouth, Burbank's Pilgrim Bookstore	203
Printers.	
Thomas Todd	229
Samuel Usher	231
George H. Walker & Co.	227
Publishers.	
Burbank, Pilgrim Bookstore, Plymouth	203
Bible Study Publishing Co.	207
The Century Co. (Fourth cover page.)	
W. F. Draper, Andover	197
W. L. Greene & Co., The Congregationalist	5, 181, 221
Houghton, Mifflin & Co.	185, 187, 189
Little, Brown & Co.	183
Lothrop Publishing Company	195
Warren F. Kellogg, New England Magazine (Second cover.)	
G. & C. Merriam Company	199
Oxford University Press	205
Perry Mason & Co., The Youth's Companion	201
Silver, Burdett & Co.	193
Small, Maynard & Co.	191
Soule Photograph Co.	175
George H. Walker & Co.	227
W. A. Wilde Company	209
REED & BARTON, Communion Cups	217
Rugs, Torrey, Bright & Capen Company	171
SHEPARD, NORWELL & CO. (Third cover page.)	
Shoes, Shepard, Norwell & Co. (Third cover page.)	
SILVER, BURDETT & CO.	193
SMALL, MAYNARD & CO.	191
SOULE PHOTOGRAPH CO.	175
Sunday-school Lessons.	
Blakeslee's Graded Sunday-school Lessons	207
Peloubet's Graded Quarterlies	209
TIFFANY GLASS AND DECORATING CO.	211
Thomas, Rev. Reuen, Books by	183
TODD, THOMAS, Printer	229
TORREY, BRIGHT & CAPEN COMPANY, Carpets and Rugs	171
Travel, H. Gaze & Sons	6
USHER, SAMUEL, Printer	231
WALKER, GEORGE H. & CO., Maps and Guide Books, etc.	227
WATERMAN, F. A., Expert Boston Guide	177
"Webster's Dictionary," G. & C. Merriam Company	199
WHEATON SEMINARY, for Young Ladies	225
WHEELER REFLECTOR CO., Church Lights	215
WILDE, W. A. COMPANY	209
YOUTH'S COMPANION, THE	201

Gilchrist & Company's
NEW BUILDING.

THIS is merely an outline of what you will see on Washington Street, of the new building now in process of erection, a few steps from Summer Street. The internal arrangements will greatly add to your comfort and facilitate you in shopping expeditions for Dry Goods. We are grateful to the multitudes of patrons from every section of New England that have contributed to our success, thus compelling us to add this new building to our establishment.

Until February first we are confined to 5, 7, 9, and 11 Winter Street.

GILCHRIST & COMPANY.

BOSTON. GARDNER MANSION.
Formerly on the site of the store of C. F. Hovey & Co.

C. F. Hovey & Co.

IMPORTERS AND
RETAILERS OF

Dry Goods

BOSTON

33 Summer Street
AND 42 Avon Street

BOSTON.   OLD SUMMER STREET.
Showing Washington Street and Park Street Church spire in the distance.

TORREY, BRIGHT & CAPEN CO.

Carpets

AND

Rugs

348-350 WASHINGTON ST.

Elbridge Torrey, Pres.   Sam'l B. Capen, Treas.

AN OLD CORNER CUPBOARD WITH ITS COLONIAL TREASURES.

HISTORICAL CHINA.

Twenty-eight views, as below, on dessert plates (9 inch) engraved for us by Wedgwood from picturesque etchings, in genuine old blue Wedgwood with foliage border; the following views: —

State House, Boston, Bulfinch front, dedicated 1795. — Old South Church. Tea Party met here 1773. — Old North Church, Salem Street. Paul Revere's Lanterns were displayed here 1775. — King's Chapel, Boston, built 1686, rebuilt 1749. — Faneuil Hall, "Cradle of Liberty," built 1742. — Site of Adams House, Boston, 1845; Lamb Tavern, 1746. — Boston Common and State House, 1836. — Harbor View of Boston from a map of 1768. — Old Brick Church, 1713, site of Joy's, now Rogers' Building. — State Street and Old State House, 1888. — Adjacent Lean-to Houses, in Quincy, Mass., each of which was the birthplace of a President of the United States. — The Public Library, Boston, 1895. — Mount Vernon, 1892, the home of Washington. — Old State House, East end, built 1657, rebuilt 1712. — Mayflower in Plymouth Harbor, 1620. — Boston Town-House, 1657, first seat of Massachusetts Government, built by Thomas Joy; burned 1711. Site, head of State Street, Boston. — Longfellow's early home, 1898, Portland, built 1783, etc.

Dessert Plates as above, **$6.00** per dozen; same if gilded edge, **$7.80**. Securely packed for shipping long distances. Visitors will find in our Art Pottery Rooms, Dinner Set Department, Hotel and Club Department, Cut Glass Department, Lamp Department, Stock Pattern Department, and on the main floor, an extensive exhibit of Jardinieres and Pedestals, Umbrella and Cane Holders, Handsome Odd Pitchers, Cafe Entree Dishes, etc.

JONES, McDUFFEE & STRATTON CO.

China, Glass, and Lamps, Wholesale and Retail.

120 Franklin Street (Corner Federal),   BOSTON, MASS.

BOSTON. MUSEUM OF FINE ARTS.

On St. James Avenue, fronting Copley Square. Founded in 1870. The present building represents the front wing of the contemplated double quadrangle. One of four sections. The Museum contains many valuable art collections, and is open to the public, under certain conditions, every day in the week.

Photographic Views...

Headquarters for Views of

BOSTON, CONCORD, PLYMOUTH,
WHITE MOUNTAINS,
NEW ENGLAND COAST, Etc.

ART PHOTOGRAPHS.

Reproductions of the Famous Works of Old and Modern Painters.

20,000 SUBJECTS IN STOCK.

Photograph Mounting ... Albums ... Picture Framing

VISITORS WELCOME.

Soule Photograph Company

338 WASHINGTON STREET,
BOSTON.   One Flight

BOSTON. THE SUN TAVERN.

An ancient landmark, situated opposite Faneuil Hall. In early Revolutionary days it was the meeting place of many of the leading men of the times.

See Boston

— intelligently — with

F. A. WATERMAN

Expert Boston Guide
(Since July, 1855)

Parties Leave at 9.30 and 2.30, Front of Park Street Church, Boston (Opposite 122 Tremont Street).

Personally conducted by Mr. Waterman.
Seeing Interesting and Historic Places.
Three-Hour Trips only Fifty Cents each.

These trips save Time, Labor, Money.
Invaluable to the Sight-seer.

F. A. WATERMAN, 10 Hamilton Place, Boston.

BOSTON. OLD STATE HOUSE.

Erected in 1748 on the site occupied by the Town House destroyed by fire the year previous. First used as a Town House, then for the courts and Colonial Legislature and for the Provincial Council; after the Revolution the meeting place of the General Court of the Commonwealth; after the town became a city it was the City Hall and for a while the post office. The building above the first floor is in custody of the Bostonian Society, and, so far as practicable, has been restored to its ancient appearance. The Society has on exhibition in the halls of the building collections of antiquarian interest.

N. J. BARTLETT & CO.

28 CORNHILL, BOSTON

ORDIALLY invite the members of the *International Congregational Council* to inspect their large and interesting collection of Books, both new and second-hand.

The five stories of our building are filled with volumes of all kinds that appeal to the scholarly taste, including

General Theological Books,
English Volumes in Choice Bindings
(MANY OF THEM RARE), AND
New English and American Books.

We are continually buying complete libraries containing rare and valuable publications. The individual books from these are offered for sale to our patrons at moderate prices.

N. J. BARTLETT & CO.,
28 Cornhill, Boston.

THE "OLD CORNER BOOKSTORE."
Built by Thomas Chase in 1712, on the site of the dwelling of Anne Hutchinson. Occupied as a bookstore since 1828.

DAMRELL & UPHAM,

"Old Corner Bookstore"

Standard and Miscellaneous Books

American and Foreign Periodicals,
Scientific, Medical, and Agricultural Works,
Bibles and Religious Publications.

283 WASHINGTON STREET,
Corner School Street,

BOSTON, MASS.

The Congregationalist Publications

CLOSET AND ALTAR
(JUST ISSUED.)

Meditations and prayers upon various themes and for special occasions. Arranged for everyday use of the individual or the family. A unique book, containing much original material, many quaint and beautiful selections and prayers from mediæval and Puritan writers, as well as from modern sources, together with those classics essential to every handbook of devotion.

200 pp., semi-flexible cover, gilt top, postpaid, $1.00.

BOOK OF THE PILGRIMAGE

The story of The Congregationalist's Pilgrimage to England and Holland. 150 illustrations and many autographs.

Sumptuous quarto, gilt top and sides, buckram, beveled, $2.00.

SERVICES. (39 Numbers.)

Sixteen pages, responsive readings and hymns with music. Each centering around one thought. These services have been phenomenally successful, about a million copies having been sold. A complete sample set sent to any address, postpaid, for 15 cents.

100 copies, 60 cents, postpaid.

THE HISTORICAL TABLETS

Proof impressions of the historical tablet on the façade of the Congregational House, suitable for framing, with a fine picture of the House and a descriptive article by Dr. E. G. PORTER, D.D.

Sent, postpaid, in mailing tube, 25 cents.

THE HANDBOOK SERIES

Published quarterly. Many valuable issues, among them:—

"THE HANDBOOK," containing daily Bible readings, prayer meeting topics, and denominational information for current year.

"CHURCH INCORPORATION." Legal information regarding this important matter, with method of procedure. (*Ten cents.*)

"THE NEW FREE CHURCH CATECHISM."

MONOGRAPHS ON PHILANTHROPIC WORK.

Single copies, 4 cents, postpaid. 100 copies, $1.25, postpaid.

The Congregationalist,

14 BEACON STREET,   BOSTON, MASS., U.S.A.

BOSTON. FANEUIL HALL.

Erected 1762-63 by the town, funds to meet its cost being raised in part by a lottery. It stands on the site of the first Faneuil Hall, the gift of Peter Faneuil, a wealthy merchant of French descent. This first hall, planned originally as a market house, was enlarged to provide a public hall, and was dedicated to "the interest of liberty and loyalty to a king under whom we enjoy this liberty." It was built in 1742 and burned in 1761. The first public meeting held in this original hall was assembled to commemorate the giver, who had suddenly died, March, 1713.

THE KINSHIP OF SOULS.
A Narrative.

BY REUEN THOMAS.

12mo. Cloth, extra. $1.50.

A very readable volume. . . . The different characters are drawn with delicacy and spirit.
— *The Advance.*

Dr. Reuen Thomas is one of the few ministers who have written a good novel. — *The Outlook.*

He takes us over familiar paths with the freshness of a new guide who knows how to reveal their hidden beauties, and he shows us how much more travelling ought to be than merely " seeing the sights." — *The Congregationalist.*

READY THIS FALL.

THE PURITAN AS A COLONIST AND A REFORMER.

BY EZRA HOYT BYINGTON, D.D.

Illustrated. 8vo. Cloth. $2.00.

This volume supplements the author's previous book, "The Puritan in England and New England," which has been pronounced by high authorities a very important contribution to the early history of New England. It will include the following chapters: I. Shakespeare and the Puritans; II. The Pilgrim as a Colonist; III. The Puritan as a Colonist; IV. John Eliot, the Apostle to the Indians; V. Jonathan Edwards and the Great Awakening.

BY THE SAME AUTHOR.

THE PURITAN IN ENGLAND AND NEW ENGLAND. With an Introduction by ALEXANDER MCKENZIE, D.D., Minister of the First Church in Cambridge, U.S.A. 8vo. Three illustrations. $2.00.

A really great book. A positive and valuable contribution to the historical literature of the Puritan in England, among the Dutch, and in New England. — *Journal of Education.*

THE CHRIST OF YESTERDAY, TO-DAY, AND FOREVER, and Other Sermons. 12mo. Cloth. $1.50.

In substance, method, and tone, the sermons are excellent. — *The Churchman.*

LITTLE, BROWN & CO., Publishers
254 Washington Street, BOSTON.

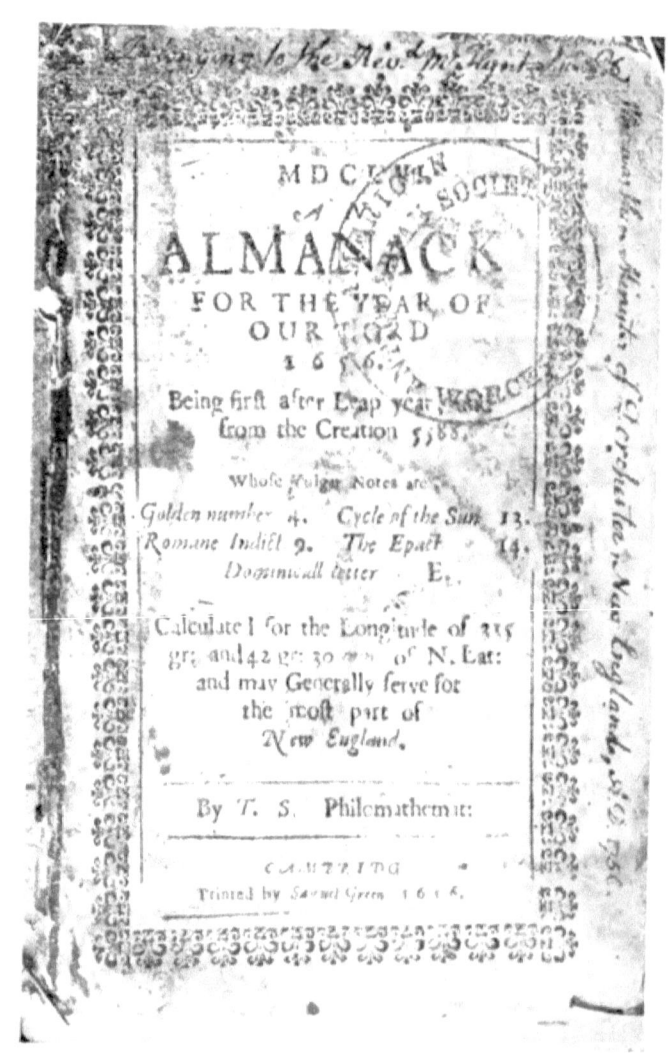

PRINTED BY SAMUEL GREEN, CAMBRIDGE, MASS., 1656.

A Great Congregationalist.

HORACE BUSHNELL

BY

THEODORE T. MUNGER, D.D.,

Author of
"Freedom and Faith," "The Appeal to Life," etc.

WITH TWO PORTRAITS. 12MO. $2.00.

Dr. Bushnell was for many years one of the brightest and clearest lights of the American pulpit. With a mind of uncommon originality, a poetic imagination, a profound love and reverence for truth, and a remarkable power of clear and forcible statement, he was of a character to illustrate and reinforce the truths he preached. He had the misfortune, or the good fortune, to be in advance of the main body of the ecclesiastical army to which he belonged; and this exposed him to the bullets of those in his rear as well as the arrows of those in front. He received both in the manliest fashion; he could truthfully say: "I have fought a good fight; I have kept the faith." And both the fighting and the keeping have given him a great name among American religious leaders, and made him a great glory to the Congregational pulpit.

Dr. Munger would seem to have been foreordained to write Dr. Bushnell's life. Having so much in common with Dr. Bushnell, so deep sympathy with his religious views and attitude, and so strong admiration of his character and worth, Dr. Munger is peculiarly fitted to interpret him to this generation, and to erect an enduring memorial to him.

Sold by all Booksellers. Sent, postpaid, by

HOUGHTON, MIFFLIN & CO., Boston.

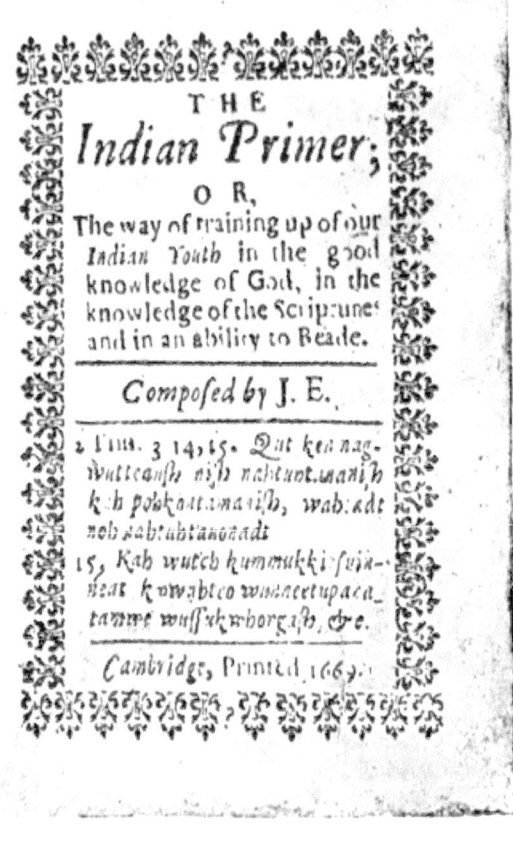

JOHN ELIOT'S INDIAN PRIMER, 1669.

Two Sterling Books
By Alexander McKenzie, D.D.

THE DIVINE FORCE IN THE LIFE OF THE WORLD.

WITH A PHOTOGRAVURE PORTRAIT. 12MO. $1.50.

This volume contains Dr. McKenzie's Lowell Institute lectures. Rev. Dr. R. S. Storrs, writing of it in *The Congregationalist*, says: "The volume is alive with fine, various, animating thought, conveyed in a literary form of singular freshness, vigor, and piquant beauty. The series of subjects presented is of vast compass, reaching from the creation to the final coming on earth of the Divine Kingdom. The fine intelligence and the liberal learning with which each is handled are always in evidence." Dr. Thomas S. Hastings in the New York *Evangelist*, after describing the work, remarks: "We close this volume refreshed and strengthened. It nerves one's faith, renews one's courage, and it fills one with a new hopefulness to read such a book as this."

A DOOR OPENED

BY

ALEXANDER McKENZIE, D.D.

WITH A PORTRAIT. 12MO, GILT TOP. $1.50.

"Dr. McKenzie's sermons 'read well.' They read wonderfully well. One who has often heard the great preacher has only to exercise memory and imagination to find in his printed sermons almost the same strange, deep, stirring, thrilling, uplifting, resistless sense of being in the grasp of a more than earthly power that so many thousands of the students of Harvard University have experienced during the past thirty years, have never forgotten and can never forget."

Sold by all Booksellers. Sent, postpaid, by

HOUGHTON, MIFFLIN & CO., Boston.

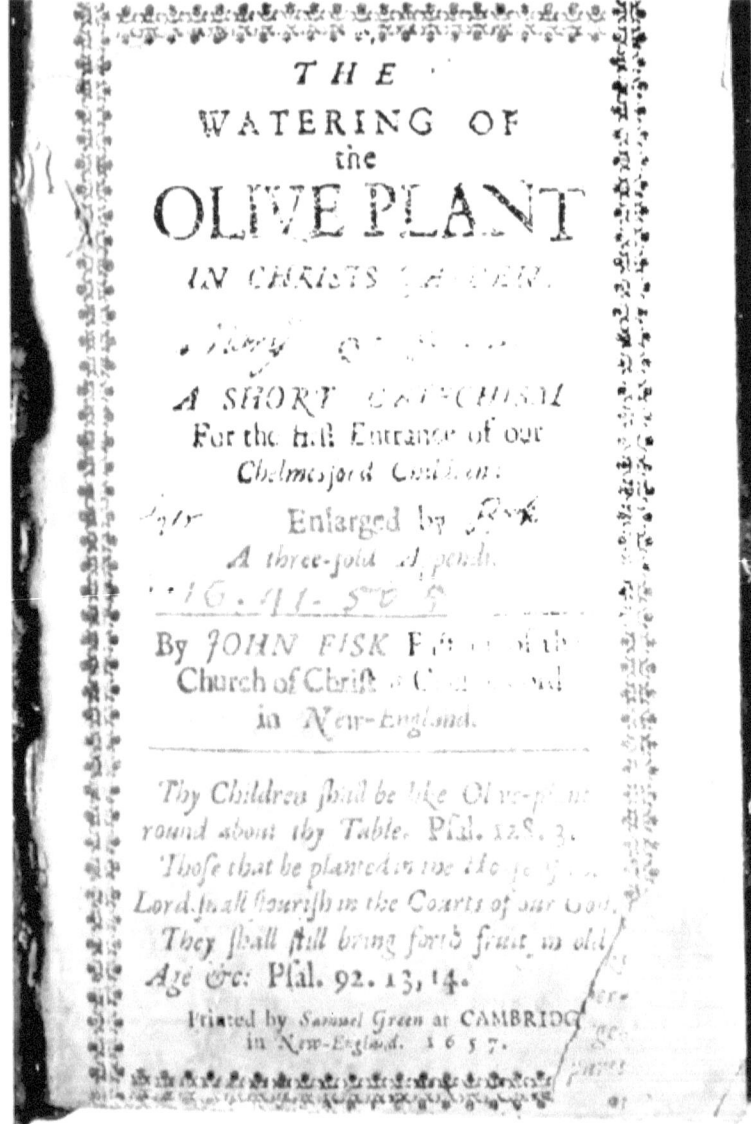

TITLE PAGE OF JOHN FISKE'S CATECHISM, 1657.
From "Beginnings of New England," published by Houghton, Mifflin & Co.

Books by the Pastor of the Old South Church,

GEORGE A. GORDON, D.D.

THE WITNESS TO IMMORTALITY IN LITERATURE, PHILOSOPHY AND LIFE.

12MO. $1.50.

"It deals with one of the most grand and solemn themes in a masterly and helpful manner." — *The Congregationalist, Boston.*

THE CHRIST OF TO-DAY.

12MO. $1.50.

"The whole book is wonderfully fresh and suggestive." — *Christian Register, Boston.*

IMMORTALITY AND THE NEW THEODICY.

16MO. $1.00.

"A discussion of uncommon breadth and thoroughness." — *The Outlook, New York.*

Sold by all Booksellers. Sent, postpaid, by

HOUGHTON, MIFFLIN & CO., Boston.

BRIEF MEMOIRS OF EMINENT AMERICANS.[1]

The Beacon Biographies.

M. A. DeWOLFE HOWE, Editor.

The Most Compact, Beautiful, Practical, and Entertaining Series of Biographies on the Market.

The aim of the series is to furnish brief, readable, and authentic accounts of the lives of those Americans whose personalities have impressed themselves most deeply on the character and history of their country. On account of the length of the more formal lives, often running into large volumes, the average busy man and woman have not the time or hardly the inclination to acquaint themselves with American biography. In the present series everything that such a reader would ordinarily care to know is given by writers of special competence, who possess in full measure the best contemporary point of view. Each volume is equipped with a frontispiece portrait, a calendar of important dates, and a brief bibliography for further reading. Finally, the volumes are printed in a form convenient for reading and for carrying handily in the pocket.

The following volumes are the first issued : —
Phillips Brooks, by the EDITOR.
David G. Farragut, by JAMES BARNES.
Robert E. Lee, by W. P. TRENT.
James Russell Lowell, by EDWARD EVERETT HALE, JR.
Daniel Webster, by NORMAN HAPGOOD.

The following are among those in preparation : —
John James Audubon, by JOHN BURROUGHS.
Edwin Booth, by CHARLES TOWNSEND COPELAND.
John Brown, by J. E. CHAMBERLIN.
Aaron Burr, by HENRY CHILDS MERWIN.
James Fenimore Cooper, by W. B. SHUBRICK CLYMER.
Frederick Douglass, by CHARLES W. CHESNUTT.
Benjamin Franklin, by LINDSAY SWIFT.
Nathaniel Hawthorne, by MRS. JAMES T. FIELDS.

PRICE, 75 CENTS.

SMALL, MAYNARD & COMPANY, Publishers
6 BEACON STREET, BOSTON.

DANVERS. OAK KNOLL, HOME OF JOHN GREENLEAF WHITTIER.

Historic Pilgrimages in New England.

Among Landmarks of Pilgrim and Puritan Days, and of the Colonial and Pre-Revolutionary Periods. By EDWIN M. BACON. 12mo, 486 pp. Over 120 illustrations. Cloth, $1.50.

A thoroughly delightful narrative of personally conducted tours to some of the most important scenes in our country's history. Historically accurate, abounding in incident, and told with all the skill of an accomplished *raconteur*.

"It is an admirable book, which will not only be a help to pilgrims, but will be a most valuable book of reference to all persons interested in our history." — *Edward Everett Hale.*

"Every library will be richer when this book is added to it. It is history localized and specialized. . . . It is, indeed, a book well wrought of American stuff and dyed with American pigments." — *The Independent, New York.*

STRONG AND HELPFUL BOOKS.

A Harmony of the Gospels for Historical Study.

By WM. ARNOLD STEVENS, D.D., and Professor ERNEST DE WITT BURTON. Quarto, 249 pp. $1.50.

This Harmony corresponds in its main divisions to the natural divisions of the life and ministry of Jesus, as indicated in the four Gospels; it exhibits the differences as well as the resemblances of the Gospels; and it is especially valuable in its arrangement of the teachings and sayings of Christ.

Doctrine and Life.

By GEORGE B. STEVENS, PH.D., D.D., Yale University. 12mo, cloth. $1.25.

"A contribution of great value towards a view of divine truth which will justify itself to the noblest ethical convictions." — *The Watchman.*

Through Death to Life.

Ten Discourses on St. Paul's great resurrection chapter. By REUEN THOMAS, D.D. 12mo, cloth. $1.25.

"A book to be read and prized; full of the light and aroma of the most precious hopes and glorious realities." — *The Advance.*

Some Aspects of the Religious Life of New England.

By GEORGE LEON WALKER, D.D. 12mo, 208 pp. $1.25.

"A vivid, but dispassionate and instructive, picture of the most important phases of New England religious life, by one familiar with the ground." — *Prof. G. P. Fisher, Yale University.*

Also superior Text-books for Schools, Academies, and Colleges.
Illustrated catalogue and descriptive circulars sent on application.

SILVER, BURDETT & COMPANY

NEW YORK.   BOSTON: CHICAGO.
219-223 Columbus Ave. (Pope B'ld'g).

From Guide to Metropolitan Boston
Copyright, 1899, Geo. H. Walker & Co.

New Books!

Tales of the Malayan Coast

By ROUNSERELLE WILDMAN,
Consul-General of the United States at Hong Kong.

$1.00

Has much of that rugged power that characterizes Kipling's Jungle Book. — *Boston Herald.*

Yesterday Framed in To-day $1.50

By "PANSY" (Mrs. G. R. Alden)

A STORY OF THE CHRIST AND HOW TO-DAY RECEIVED HIM.

This new book by Pansy is an inspiration. Into the to-day of railroads and telegraphs, phonographs, and electric lights, she brings a central figure — Jesus the Christ.

WE SHOULD BE PLEASED TO HAVE YOU CALL AND EXAMINE OUR BOOKS, OR TO SEND FOR NEW PORTRAIT CATALOGUE.

Lothrop Publishing Company

530 ATLANTIC AVENUE,
BOSTON, MASS.

BOSTON. BUNKER HILL MONUMENT.

Commemorating the battle of 17 June, 1775. Begun 1825; completed 1842. Corner stone laid by the Marquis de Lafayette. Orator of the occasion, Daniel Webster. Base 30 feet square. Height 220 feet. Cost met by popular subscription.

ANDOVER PUBLICATIONS

Text-books, Commentaries.

The Catalogue of Andover Publications embraces many valuable

HELPS IN BIBLICAL STUDY,

Both for general readers and for the special use of Clergymen and Theological Students, such as **Works on the Evidences, Defence and Illustration of Christian Truth, Devotional Books, Essays in Philosophy and Theology, Church History, Hermeneutics,** by Learned Professors.

Commentaries by some of the most eminent English and American Scholars, such as Bishop C. J. Ellicott on the Pauline Epistles; Dr. E. Henderson on the Minor Prophets, Jeremiah and Lamentations; Prof. J. B. Lightfoot on Galatians; Prof. James G. Murphy on the First Four Books of the Old Testament, and on Psalms and Daniel; Dr. J. J. Stewart Perowne on the Psalms; Prof. Moses Stuart on parts of the Old and New Testaments; The Lowell Hebrew Club on the Book of Esther: Prof. Geo. H. Schodde's Book of Enoch.

Harmonies of the Gospels in English and in Greek, by Prof. Frederic Gardiner.

The Indispensable New Testament Greek Grammars of Buttmann and Winer, translated by Prof. J. Henry Thayer. These two New Testament Grammars are, by special arrangement, offered for a short time at less than half price. Terms given on application.

Elementary Hebrew Grammar, and other Text-books, for College and School use. Works by Profs. George L. Cary, J. W. Haley, Samuel Harris, Joseph Haven, Thomas Hill, E. A. Park, Austin Phelps, Enoch Pond, William G. T. Shedd, Alexander Wheelock Thayer, William S. Tyler, W. H. Vibbert, Archbishop Whately, G. Frederick Wright, Judge Charles B. Morrison, and others.

Just published, SEQUEL TO ANNALS OF FIFTY YEARS. History of Abbot Academy from 1879-1892, by Miss Philena McKeen. Price, $2.25 net.

For full particulars send for a Descriptive Catalogue.

Discount given to Clergymen.

W. F. DRAPER, Publisher, ANDOVER, MASS.

BOSTON. MASSACHUSETTS CHARITABLE MECHANICS ASSOCIATION BUILDING.

The Society was founded in 1795. Its original objects were to relieve the wants of unfortunate mechanics and their families; to promote inventions and improvements in mechanic arts; to assist young mechanics by loans of money; and to establish schools and libraries for use of apprentices. The first president of the association was Paul Revere. This building, erected in 1880-81, covers a space of about seven acres, and is utilized for the regular triennial exhibition of the association and for other large gatherings. One of the halls has a seating capacity of 8,000.

WEBSTER'S INTERNATIONAL DICTIONARY

of ENGLISH, Biography, Geography, Fiction, etc.

IT EXCELS in the ease with which the eye finds the word sought; in accuracy of definition; in effective methods of indicating pronunciation; in terse and comprehensive statements of facts and in practical use as a working dictionary.

A FEW SELECTED COMMENDATIONS.

Rev. Lyman Abbott, D.D., Editor of The Outlook.
Webster has always been the favorite in our household and I have seen no reason to transfer my allegiance to any of his competitors.

President Charles W. Eliot, LL.D., of Harvard University.
It is a wonderfully compact storehouse of accurate information.

Rev. L. D. Bevan, LL.D., of Melbourne.
It is, in its way, easily the first of the great dictionaries of our language.

President James B. Angell, LL.D., of University of Michigan.
The International must easily and securely hold its place.

Rev. Charles Cuthbert Hall, D.D., of Union Theological Seminary.
Its arrangement facilitates rapid reference; the definitions combine clearness with conciseness.

President Wm. D. Hyde, D.D., of Bowdoin College.
The International Dictionary is all that could be desired.

Prof. Edward Dowden, of Dublin University.
It may be said with fresh emphasis that it is the best practical English dictionary extant.

The Congregationalist.
All will find it a scholarly, practical, comprehensive, and thoroughly trustworthy work.

Specimen pages sent on application.

G. & C. Merriam Company,
Publishers,
SPRINGFIELD, MASS., U.S.A.

BOSTON. CITY HALL.

NO matter who was the clergyman, or whether the homily were short or long, Mr. Gladstone listened continuously, says the Rev. Charles Fox, as quoted in

The Youth's Companion.

The last piece of literary work done by the great statesman was an article written for The Companion.

Men of eminence on both sides of the Atlantic are frequent contributors to this paper, which every week in the year brings an influence of cheer, inspiration and help into more than half a million homes.

VISITORS WELCOME.

The various departments of the Companion Building are freely open, and a guide is appointed to show visitors all the work of getting the paper out, from printing to mailing. On the fifth floor is this year's Prize Exhibition of Amateur Photographs.

Perry Mason & Company,
201 Columbus Avenue, Boston, Mass.

PLYMOUTH. W. F. HALSALL'S PAINTING OF THE MAYFLOWER.

"IN PLYMOUTH

The Land of the Pilgrims"

Delegates are invited to a...

FREE EXHIBITION

—AT—

BURBANK'S PILGRIM BOOKSTORE

of Paintings of historic scenes in Pilgrim Life. Among them are...

Plymouth Colony in 1622. The Old Meeting House Fort, 1621.
The Ship Mayflower. Governor Bradford's House in 1621.
Coats-of-Arms of Mayflower Families.

☛ BURBANK'S PILGRIM BOOKSTORE is the headquarters for Pilgrim Souvenirs, and the publishing house for Pilgrim Literature. Histories, Guide-books, Stories about the Pilgrims, Photographs, Coats-of-Arms. *Lantern Slides* for illustrating Pilgrim Lectures. Send stamp for Burbank's Illustrated Catalogue.

FIFTY PLYMOUTH PICTURES.— If you want to know just *what to see* in Plymouth, and *how to see it*, send for

"HISTORIC PLYMOUTH."

A handsome book descriptive of the historic points and localities famous in the story of the Pilgrims. It is illustrated with fifty half-tone engravings, and sketches in pen and ink. A beautiful cover design in color by Hallowell, of John Alden and Priscilla. The Price, only twenty-five cents, at

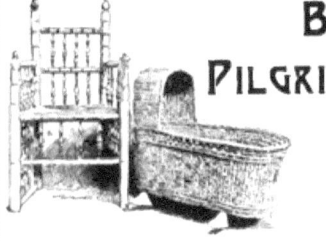

BURBANK'S
PILGRIM BOOKSTORE,

19 and 21 COURT STREET,

PLYMOUTH, MASS.

PLYMOUTH. ONE OF THE CROOKED HIGHWAYS.
(*See pages 77-87, Boston Book.*)

RECENTLY PUBLISHED

Large Type Edition

The Revised Bible
With References.

At prices from $1.25 upward. Also, the

Original American Revised Bible

With the readings and renderings authorized by the American Revision Companies of 1870-1884, incorporated in the text, and with **Copyright Marginal References**, at prices from $1.25 upward.

NOW READY! Twenty New Copyright Editions of the

"Oxford" Teachers' Bibles
And Authorized American Edition.

With New Helps, Maps, and 124 Full-Page Plates.

The Best Paper

The Best Printing

The Best Binding

The Helps *The Christian Advocate*, Nashville, says: "The helps are real helps. Unlike those in many of the cheap Bibles, they are not simply thrown together in hodge-podge fashion, but represent the freshest and ablest work of the foremost modern scholars."

The Illustrations *The Sunday-School Times*, Sept. 17, 1898, says: "In this department this Bible is probably *far superior* to any other of those commonly called teachers' Bibles."

In Actual Use "I want to emphasize the value of this book, since I know it by personal experience. The helps of the Oxford Bible are really what they are called. . . . On the whole, I think it is the best for the average teacher."— *Rev.* Dr. A. F. Schauffler.

For Sale by all booksellers. Send for catalog.

Oxford University Press American Branch

91 and 93 Fifth Avenue, New York.

PLYMOUTH. BURIAL HILL.
(See page 81, Boston Book.)

THE BIBLE STUDY UNION (or BLAKESLEE)
Graded Sunday-School Lessons

The **ONLY LESSONS** by which a school can be thoroughly graded.

The **ONLY LESSONS** that give complete and connected courses of study.

The **ONLY LESSONS** that have courses specially adapted to the Primary Department, the Main School, and the Bible Classes.

First issued in 1891. Now used in almost all Evangelical denominations, and translated by missionaries into SPANISH, TURKISH, ARMENIAN, SYRIAC, TELUGU, BENGALI, JAPANESE, and CHINESE.

Used in the following leading Congregational Churches: —

FIRST, Cambridge, Mass.	Rev. Alexander McKenzie, D.D.
MOUNT VERNON, Boston.	Rev. Samuel E. Herrick, D.D.
CENTRAL, Boston.	Rev. Edward L. Clark, D.D.
BRIGHTON, Boston.	Rev. A. A. Berle, D.D.
HARVARD, Brookline, Mass.	Rev. Reuen Thomas, D.D.
CENTRAL, Worcester, Mass.	Rev. Daniel Merriman, D.D.
SOUTH, Springfield, Mass.	Rev. Philip H. Moxom, D.D.
CENTRAL, Providence, R. I.	Rev. Edward C. Moore, D.D.
FIRST, New London, Ct.	Rev. S. Leroy Blake, D.D.
ASYLUM HILL, Hartford, Ct.	Rev. Joseph H. Twitchell.
FIRST, New Haven, Ct.	Rev. Newman Smyth, D.D.
UNITED, New Haven, Ct.	Rev. Theodore T. Munger, D.D.
REDEEMER, New Haven, Ct.	Rev. Watson L. Phillips, D.D.
TOMPKINS AVENUE, Brooklyn, N.Y.	Rev. R. R. Meredith, D.D.
PLYMOUTH, Brooklyn, N.Y.	Rev. Newell D. Hillis, D.D.
MONTCLAIR, Montclair, N. J.	Rev. A. H. Bradford, D.D.
EUCLID AVENUE, Cleveland, O.	Rev. Caspar W. Hiatt, D.D.
PLYMOUTH, Cleveland, O.	Rev. Livingston L. Taylor.
PLYMOUTH, Milwaukee, Wis.	Rev. Judson Titsworth, D.D.
PLYMOUTH, Minneapolis, Minn.	Rev. L. H. Hallock, D.D.

And many others.

These lessons are issued in six series, three biographical and three historical, each set of three covering the entire Bible. Each series has three courses and seven grades, carefully adapted to the capacity and needs of all classes, from the youngest to the oldest.

By the use of these lessons, young people in the ordinary years of Sunday-school life gain a familiar acquaintance with the Bible as a whole, and a connected and well-arranged knowledge of all its principal events and teachings.

Specimen copies free. Address, **THE BIBLE STUDY PUBLISHING CO.**, 21 Bromfield Street, BOSTON, MASS.

PLYMOUTH.

A SEASIDE PASTURE.

(See pages 77–87. *Boston Book.*)

W. A. WILDE COMPANY,

Sunday-school Publishers.

 E carry a full line of Sunday-school Helps and Requisites of all kinds. We shall be glad to send our Catalogues, upon application, giving description and prices of ...

PELOUBET'S SELECT NOTES.

GRADED QUARTERLIES.

Six Grades, including our new *Home Department Quarterly*, and Four Teacher's Editions.

LIBRARY BOOKS.

Our list of superior books for Sunday-school Libraries includes several volumes that have created widespread comment because of their distinctive excellences. They are offered to librarians as being striking examples of progressive bookmaking, as well as being the best literary effort of some of America's leading authors. It has been said that their appearance "marked a new era in Sunday-school Library Books."

Illustrated Papers and Song Books.
Sunday-school Pictures illustrating the Life of Christ.
Concert Exercises.
Golden Texts, Record Books of all kinds, Catechisms, Reward Cards, etc.

W. A. WILDE COMPANY,

BOSTON.   CHICAGO.

MEMORIAL WINDOW IN CENTRAL CONGREGATIONAL CHURCH, BOSTON.

(*Designed and executed by the Tiffany Glass and Decorating Co.*)

Artistic Memorials.

OUR memorial windows are made of

Tiffany Favrile Glass

which is produced exclusively at our own furnace, and cannot be obtained from other makers or used by any other artists. In range, depth, and brilliancy of color it has never been equaled, and when we employ it in window work the greatest care is exercised in selecting the pieces in order that we may obtain the desired effect both in color and texture. The selection is made by a trained artisan, under the supervision of an artist. Special designs and estimates submitted.

Historical Booklet (Illustrated) sent upon request.

The following are among the notable Congregational Churches in which there are examples of our work:—

Central Congregational Church, Boston, Mass.
Mount Vernon Congregational Church, Boston, Mass.
Harvard Street Congregational Church, Brookline, Mass.
Shepard Memorial Church, Cambridge, Mass.
Walnut Avenue Congregational Church, Roxbury, Mass.
Eliot Congregational Church, Newton, Mass.
Winter Hill Congregational Church, Somerville, Mass.
Congregational Church, Wakefield, Mass.
Congregational Church, Plymouth, Mass.

TIFFANY STUDIOS
Tiffany Glass and Decorating Co.
333-341 FOURTH AVENUE,
NEW YORK.

SALEM. PEABODY INSTITUTE — ACADEMY OF SCIENCE.
(*See page 66, Boston Book.*)

MENEELY BELL COMPANY

Troy, N. Y., and
177 Broadway, New York City

... MANUFACTURE ...

Superior Church Bells

The bell in the tower of the New Old South Church, Boston, was made at this foundry, and the finest Congregational churches everywhere have the bells of the MENEELY BELL COMPANY.

SALEM. CHESTNUT STREET.
(*See pages 61-75, Boston Book.*)

OUR CHURCH LIGHTS

Are Unequaled for

Beauty, Brilliancy, Economy, and Durability.

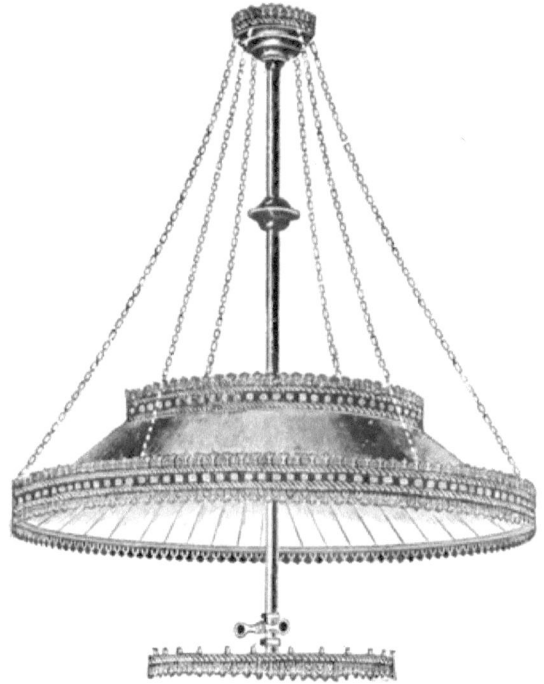

Numerous Styles for Oil, Gas, and Electricity.

In writing for estimates and prices, state length,
breadth, and height of room to be lighted.

WHEELER REFLECTOR CO.

18 to 24 Washington Street,
BOSTON, MASS. ... ...

ILLUSTRATED CATALOGUES FREE.

ROXBURY. WALNUT AVENUE CHURCH.
REV. A. H. PLUME, D.D., *Pastor*.
Organized in 1870; present edifice built in 1886-89.

Individual Communion Services.

E would invite special attention to the large assortment of designs of Cups and Trays or Stands for serving now manufactured by us. Cups are furnished in either Glass or Silver Plate.

Churches considering the adoption of the Individual Communion Cup should examine our patterns and procure our prices before placing order.

Illustrations and prices furnished on application.

REED & BARTON,
TAUNTON, MASS.

41 Union Square .. New York City .. 6 Maiden Lane.

BOSTON. SHAWMUT CHURCH.
REV. W. T. MCELVEEN, PH.D., *Pastor*.

Organized in 1845; present church building, seating 1,500 people, dedicated February 11, 1864.

THE SHAWMUT CHURCH ORGAN
of 55 speaking stops — electric — is a late example of our work.

Austin Organ Company

415-425 DORCHESTER AVENUE

BOSTON

Building Exclusively the Highest Type of Modern Organ...

THE
AUSTIN UNIVERSAL WIND CHEST SYSTEM WITH AUSTIN ELECTRIC AND TUBULAR PNEUMATIC ACTION.

(All patented in the United States, England, and Canada.)

Specialists in Pure Tone Production.

Send for "The Modern Organ" and other descriptive matter.

"CORONATION ORGAN."

Owned by Oliver Holden, a carpenter, of Charlestown (born 1765), and on which he composed the familiar tune "Coronation." The makers of the organ were Astor & Company, Cornhill, London.

The Congregationalist

ERVICES

Each Service an Order of Worship, including Responsive Readings, Hymns *with Music,* Prayers, and all necessary directions to secure the hearty co-operation of the congregation with the leader. Sixteen pages.

ONE MILLION COPIES SOLD.

39 Numbers Now Ready.

FIRST SERIES, 1-20. 1 — Thanksgiving. 2 — Pilgrim Fathers. 3 — Christmastide. 4 — New Year. 9 — Passiontide. 10 — Easter. 14 — Memorial Day. 15 — Children's Sunday. 16 — National. *Eventide Services:* — 5 — Forgiveness of Sins. 6 — Trust in God. 7 — Days of Thy Youth. 8 — House of Our God. 11 — Homeland. 12 — Humility. 13 — God in Nature. *General Worship:* — 17 — "Abide with us." 18 — "Eternal light of light." 19 — "I will extol Thee." 20 — "God be with us for the night is closing."

SECOND SERIES, 21-26. 21 — "I Am." 22 — "I Am the Bread of Life." 23 — "I Am the Light of the World." 24 — "I Am the Good Shepherd." 25 — "I Am the Way, the Truth, the Life." 26 — "I Am the Living One."

THIRD SERIES, 27-33. 27 — The Master and His Disciples. 28 — Whitsuntide. 29 — Simon Peter. 30 — James. 31 — John. 32 — Paul. 33 — An Order of Morning Worship.

FOURTH SERIES, 34-39. 34 — Forefather's Day. 35 — Songs of the Advent and Nativity. 36 — Palm Sunday. 37 — The Saints in Light. 38 — Thanksgiving for Harvest-tide. 39 — Epiphany.

Price, Sixty Cents, Postage Prepaid.

.*. Complete set of samples, 39 numbers, 15 cents, postpaid.

The Congregationalist,

14 BEACON STREET,   BOSTON, MASS., U.S.A.

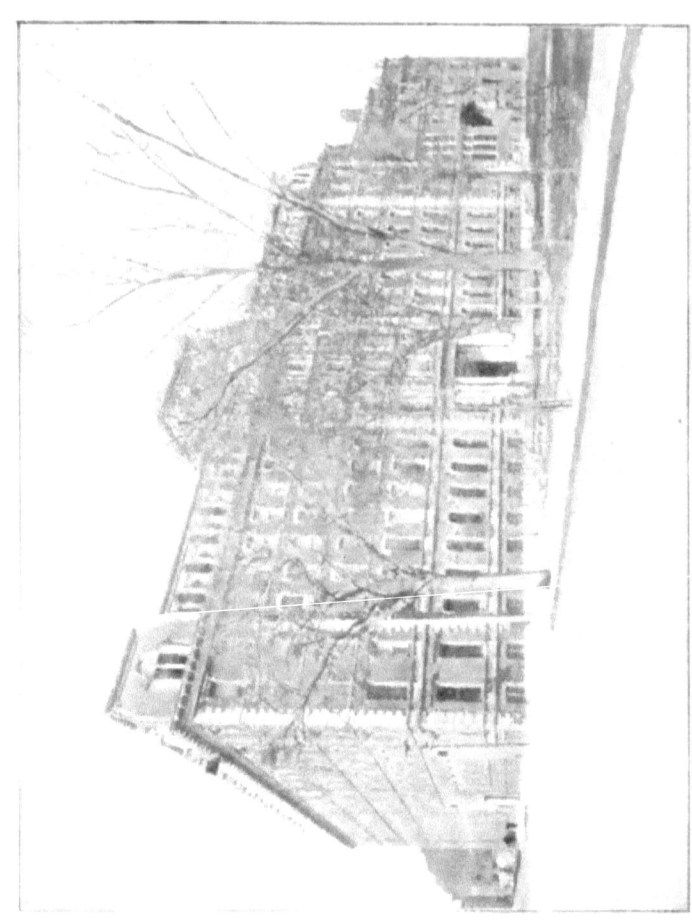

BOSTON. NEW ENGLAND CONSERVATORY OF MUSIC.

NEW ENGLAND CONSERVATORY OF MUSIC

FRANKLIN SQUARE,
BOSTON, MASS.

The Leading Conservatory in America

OFFERS A COMPLETE AND
PRACTICAL MUSICAL EDUCATION

Strangers in the city are cordially invited to visit the institution and become personally acquainted with its location and adaptation to the needs of musical students.

Fall term opens Thursday, September 14, 1899.

Pupils may enter to advantage at any time.

GEORGE W. CHADWICK, *Musical Director.*

For prospectus and full information, address

FRANK W. HALE, *General Manager.*

NORTON, MASS. WHEATON SEMINARY (FOUNDED 1834).

See opposite page for general view of

WHEATON SEMINARY

FOR

Young Women.

A CHRISTIAN HOME SCHOOL

(unsectarian) which aims to furnish the best facilities for a full and symmetrical development of mind and character. The limited number of pupils permits that familiar personal intercourse with the teachers upon which the formation of correct habits so largely depends, and it is the endeavor of the teachers that a constant and pervasive Christian influence shall be felt throughout the school.

Special care is given to health and physical training. Buildings are equipped with a perfect sanitary system, steam heat, and electric lights.

Sixty-fifth year begins September 13, 1899. Advanced courses for high school graduates and others not wishing full college course; also college preparatory and special. Advantages in art, music, elocution. Gymnasium, golf, tennis, basket ball, etc. Beautifully and healthfully situated, with extensive grounds, 28 miles from Boston.

By arrangement with the President or Trustees,* the tuition of daughters of clergymen and missionaries may be wholly or in part remitted. The Seminary is endowed and a limited number of scholarships is provided.

FOR CIRCULAR AND VIEWS, ADDRESS

Rev. SAMUEL V. COLE, D.D., President,

NORTON, MASS.

*Rev. A. H. Plumb, D.D., Boston, President of Trustees.

SOUTH SUDBURY. "THE WAYSIDE INN."

The Red Horse Tavern, built in 1683 by David Howe and kept as a tavern by four generations of his family until 1860, and then occupied as a private house. It is again open as an inn, and has been furnished throughout by the owner and landlord, E. K. Lemon, with rare antique furniture. Longfellow has made the place famous in his "Tales of The Wayside Inn," and in the parlor and taproom of the fine old house the friends gathered more than ever,— Longfellow, Parsons, Luigi Monti, Ole Bull, and others. Many other famous people have visited the house, and of course there are Lafayette and Washington rooms.

Geo. H. Walker & Co.

Lithographers,
Publishers,
Engravers,
Printers.

...SEND FOR ESTIMATES.

Pocket Maps for Cycling, Driving, and Walking,
Pocket City Maps,
Pocket Railroad Maps,
Pocket Electric Railway Maps,
Wall Maps of States,
Counties, Cities, and of the World.

ATLASES.

Send for Descriptive Catalogue. Special maps to order.

Geo. H. Walker & Co.

160 Tremont Street, OPPOSITE BOSTON COMMON, Boston, Mass.

SOUTH DUXBURY. THE STANDISH COTTAGE.

Built in 1666 by Alexander Standish, son of Capt. Miles Standish. It contains many of the timbers, doors, and latches, as well as the hearthstone, of the Captain's own house, which were saved from the ruins when the latter was burned after his death and while occupied by his son.

"The" Congregational Printer

THOMAS TODD

Book and Job Printer
Number 14 Beacon
Street   Boston

HAVE been in business thirty-six years. Have constantly received flattering acknowledgments from my customers, and can confidently guarantee that all work intrusted to me will be executed in the most approved manner.

Refer by permission to the publishers of "The Congregationalist," having been connected with the mechanical department of that paper for fifty years.

My facilities are continually increasing for the printing of

> LIBRARY CATALOGUES,
> CHURCH HISTORIES,
> CHURCH CREEDS,
> PROGRAMMES,
> SERMONS,

and all other work needed by Religious Societies; while for

> COMMERCIAL PRINTING,

in all its branches, I keep fully abreast of the demands of the most cultivated taste.

Prices very low.

Electrotyping and Stereotyping on reasonable terms.

THOMAS TODD,
Number 14 Beacon Street (Congregational House),
BOSTON, MASS.

Telephone, 601 Haymarket.

THE ALDEN HOUSE.

DUXBURY.

Built about 1660, and now occupied by one of the seventh generation. It was the third house on the homestead lot of John and Priscilla Alden, and was built by their grandson. Near by is a stream still known by the name the Pilgrims gave it — Blue Fish River.

Established in 1881

Samuel Usher
Printer

171 DEVONSHIRE STREET

BOSTON, MASS.

Book Composition and Presswork
    Lithographing and Engraving
        Stereotyping and Electrotyping
Church Histories and Manuals
    Mercantile and Catalogue Printing
        Sunday-school Text-books and Periodicals
        Law Printing of all kinds

> Printer to the American Board of Commissioners for Foreign Missions for fourteen years, and to the Congregational Sunday-School and Publishing Society since 1884.

The generous patronage with which I have been favored has enabled me to provide a large equipment of machinery and material for the execution of a high grade of work at reasonable rates. Only skilled and competent workmen employed.

> When in need of anything in my line kindly advise by mail or telephone. Estimates or other information cheerfully furnished.

Greater Country
Greatest Store...

AN Old-fashioned Country Store, which is supposed to contain a little of everything, is a great curiosity. Ours is an Old-fashioned Country Store on a gigantic scale, carrying everything usually found in a country store, and a fine Lunch Room in addition. We have,

> A Dry Goods Department,
> A Grocery Department,
> A Boot and Shoe Department,
> A Hat and Cap Department,
> A Furniture Department,
> A Crockery Department,
> A Stationery Department,
> A Hardware Department,
> A Medical Department,
> A Kitchen Goods Department,
> A Carpet Department,
> A Decorated China Department,
> ... And many others.

Visit our Excellent Spa on the Ninth Floor.

HOUGHTON & DUTTON,

Tremont, Beacon, and Somerset Streets, and Pemberton Square,   ... BOSTON.

www.ingramcontent.com/pod-product-compliance
Lightning Source LLC
Chambersburg PA
CBHW021825230426
43669CB00008B/873